on the necessity of
BESTIALIZING THE HUMAN FEMALE

MARGOT SIMS

South End Press   Boston, MA

Grateful acknowledgement is made to the following for permission to reprint copyrighted material.
    Impact Press: portion from *The Barnum-Cinderella World of Publishing.* Copyright © 1971 by Alex Jackinson

typesetting, design, and production by Ellen Herman and the South End Press Collective
cover design by Sheila Walsh

Library of Congress number: 82-61146
ISBN 0-89608-150-8 (paper)
ISBN 0-89608-151-6 (cloth)

SOUTH END PRESS/302 Columbus Ave./Boston, MA 02116

Contents

Preface

I came from a normal family with a normal family life. I grew up with my step-father, my mother, and my sister and brother, Janny and Jonny, who were twins. My step-father had a hairy body, a few yellow teeth, and a nasty disposition. I had always thought he was illiterate, but when I was ten I discovered a large assortment of books in his fishing tackle box. Unfortunately, my mother snatched them away from me and hid them before I could tell what they were about.

My mother had a diminutive frame, a beatific smile, and a gentle nature. She read stories to me whenever I asked and played the piano for hours at a time on weekends when Pop went fishing.

When they were little, Janny and Jonny shared an interest in animals. Jonny used to torture them, and Janny nursed them back to health. During adolescence, their interests changed. Jonny spent almost no time in the house, and twice hurled heavy objects at me when I came upon him playing with his penis in the garage. Janny became prone to tears, wrote in a diary for hours every day, and insisted on privacy in the bathroom (but not in the garage).

As I look back on it, it may have been during this period that I first got an inkling that there was some kind of difference between girls and boys—other than the obvious one, I mean. I knew Pop and Jonny had penises that they loved to watch bob up and down in the bathtub on the rare occasions when they bathed. But I had a feeling there was something else, something I couldn't put my finger on.

My teenage years were no more remarkable than my childhood. During high school I went steady with a boy named Tommy, and he usually went steady with me too. I used to love watching him work out in the weight room after school while I did his homework.

Tommy and I broke up in April of our senior year because I had stayed home one weekend writing a term paper for him so he could attend a Christian youth conference. When I learned that he had actually spent the weekend drinking with some friends and having sexual relations with two older women, I became angry. Tommy told me I was prudish and nosey and never called me again, even though I wrote him several letters of apology. I was disappointed that he hadn't been more sensitive to my point of view and more forgiving about my anger.

During the hours I was waiting by the telephone for Tommy to call, I couldn't help feeling that there might actually be some difference between males and females. Still, my feeling was no more than a vague impression.

In my senior year of college, I married. Life with Herb prompted me to give this recurrent feeling more careful attention. As a science major in college, I had learned to perform careful research and compile complete data before reaching conclusions. By the time Herb ran off with a nineteen-year-old hair stylist, two years and eight months after our marriage, I had learned that he drank an average of four beers before dinner; ate his dinner in an average of nine gulps, 0.5 words, and six belches; watched television for an average of three hours and seven minutes per day; had intercourse with me every third night for an average of ninety-two seconds, with an average of fourteen penile thrusts; and slept for an average of six hours and thirty-nine minutes per night during which he snored an average of two hours and sixteen minutes and emitted an average of seven farts.

On the basis of this data I began to suspect that the difference I had long sensed between men and women was a real one. For several years after my divorce I tried to solve the riddle. Just what was the elusive "difference" that I detected between male and female human beings? I decided that only an exhaustive scientific study of the natures of men and women—particularly their sexual natures—could answer that riddle.

In pursuit of the answer, I founded the Center for the Study of Human Types, and began research on human beings and other animals. The Center has been in operation for over eight years now, and our studies have led us—reluctantly but unavoidably—to the conclusions you will find in the coming pages.

Margot Sims
August 24, 1982
Bleeding Heart, Nebraska

ii

Introduction

Since 1973 at the Center for the Study of Human Types in Bleeding Heart, Nebraska, my able staff and I have conducted basic laboratory research, performed searching psychological inquiries, and investigated pertinent sociological phenomena on over two hundred species of animals to determine the nature of humanness.* Our inquiry has exposed a scientific fact of a delicate nature. I refer to the difference in the evolutionary development of male and female humans, to the undeniable fact that the female type has attained a significantly higher rung on the evolutionary ladder than her male counterpart.**

My own feeling is that the differences between the two types of humans are so great that it is not proper to consider them as members of the same species. Recent findings clearly point to there being not just one species, *Homo sapiens,* but two: *Homo veridis* (true human) and *Homo bestias* (beast human). (Figure I.1)

Roughly speaking, the true human/beast human distinction is a female/male distinction respectively, though this is not strictly the case. A few males display many of the traits we attribute to true humans, and we find beastly qualities in some numbers of women. My own studies indicate a 96% beast human and 4% true human

---

* Visitors are welcome at the Center, which lies on a vast tract of land in south central Nebraska that formerly housed a seminary for the Order of the Most Precious Bleeding Heart. The cloisters provide comfortable accommodations for guests, my staff, and me; the chapel makes a fine stable; the well-lighted rectory is a splendid studio for filming animal copulations; the confessionals provide privacy for our masturbation studies; and the self-flagellation chambers are perfect for our sado-masochism research.

** When I use the terms "high" and "low," "refined" and "coarse," "admirable" and "despicable," "good" and "bad," in this book, I don't mean to suggest one to be preferable to the other. It would be presumptuous of me to imply that it's good to be good or bad to be bad. When I refer to the female as "superior" and to the male as "inferior," I don't wish to attach praise to the one or disgrace to the other. When one compares true humans and beast humans in these matters and feels superior or inferior to someone else, he or she is just displaying his or her own pettiness. (But then, who am I so say it's wrong to be petty?)

incidence among males, and a 13% beast human and 87% true
human incidence among females. But these are ballpark figures,
and there is much controversy on this issue.

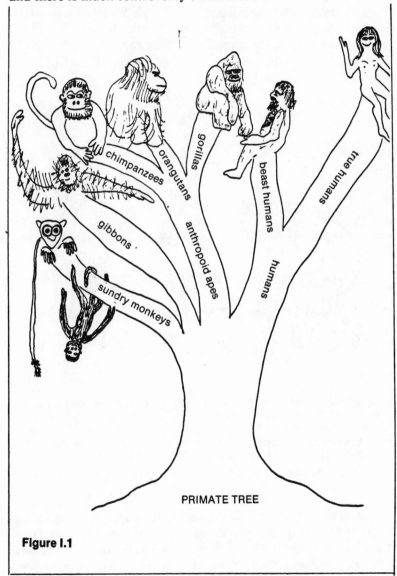

PRIMATE TREE

Figure I.1

I am not the first to have pointed out the evolutionary disparity between men and women. As early as the Sixth Century A.D. at the Synod of Macon, the Church Fathers debated whether woman was really human, and thus possessed of a soul, or merely animal and soulless. Early in this century, the German writer Max Funke called women "semi-humans," regarding them as a missing link half-way between man and the anthropoid apes. (Figure I-2)

Figure I.2   Max Funke, 20th century German writer, believed woman might well be the "missing link" between the anthropoid ape and man. (Based on this evidence of his inability to rank items in logical sequence, psychologists at the Center estimate that Funke's I.Q. was probably between 80 and 85.)

If untutored Gila monsters were to rank species in the order of evolutionary development, there is no doubt that they would rank themselves Number One. Likewise, when untutored men have grasped the evolutionary disparity between themselves and women, they have almost without exception reversed the proper order.

However, Charles Darwin, in his masterpiece *The Descent of Man,* bordered on recognizing the proper ranking of the two sexes: "There can be little doubt that the greater size and strength of man, *in comparison with woman,* together with his broader shoulders, more developed muscles, rugged outline of body, his greater courage and pugnacity, are all due in chief part to inheritance from *his half-human ancestors."* (Emphasis is mine.) I could hardly have said it better myself.

But even Darwin was at a distinct disadvantage when trying to decipher the evolutionary order of species. He did not have all the necessary scientific facts. Now, for the first time, we do have all the facts, facts which prove that a significant evolutionary gap unquestionably exists between men and women. The only remaining controversy is over exactly how great the disparity between the two human types is.

At one extreme are the scientists who contend that men and women are not only different species, but that men are not really human at all. These scientists prefer to call men *beast humanoids (Homonoido bestias),* indicating that they are beasts who resemble humans in certain superficial respects. I disagree. These scientists are overlooking two very important aspects of the beast human: (1) He uses language, and (2) he has an opposable thumb. These are human-determinant features, just as mammary glands are a mammal-determinant feature. The male human is unquestionably, if tenuously, human. (Figure I-3)

At the other extreme are those who believe the differences between the human sexes are not great enough to warrant designation as separate species. They regard men and women simply as different *varieties* of the same species, *Homo sapiens,* just as the Chihuahua and the collie are different varieties of dog, *Canis familiaris.* My own position is a moderate one between these two extremes.

However, if after reading the scientific facts contained in the first three chapters of this book, any readers are still unable to be objective enough to accept the conclusion that two species comprise humankind, I ask those readers not to be concerned with their psychological blocks, but to continue to read the remainder of the work. The problems we are dealing with and the solutions we are seeking are the same regardless of whether we are dealing with species or varieties.

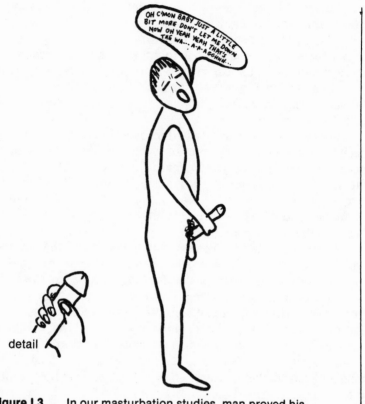

Figure I.3   In our masturbation studies, man proved his humanness again and again by his (1) use of language, and (2) opposable thumb.

Whatever the evolutionary disparity between male and female types amounts to, one important fact remains unaltered: *There is an urgent need in our world for a lower type of female human than is presently common.* In *The Descent of Man*, Charles Darwin described the millions of years it took for man to descend from his ape ancestors. But we don't have that kind of time anymore. The descent of woman must be hasty. The very highly evolved women that populate the earth today will not long remain viable in their present environment and company, and the disturbances resulting from their presence pose serious dangers to themselves and to the rest of humankind.

chapter 1

The Argument
from Design

Measuring the Evolutionary Gap

One's initial impulse is to look at man's opposable thumb, his facility with language, and his fine long penis and conclude that he's a pretty sophisticated creature in relation to other animals. But on closer inspection, as we will demonstrate in our first three chapters, many creatures—the giant scallop and the skunk among them—outrank man in evolutionary status, and he only barely outdistances the three-toed sloth and the weasel.

We can ascertain exactly how great the evolutionary gap is between beast humans and true humans by comparing them with dozens of other animals on various evolutionarily significant features, such as breeding habits and coital behavior. By the end of Chapter 3, we will have investigated thirteen such evolutionary features in detail and have a very solid data base for our conclusions about relative evolutionary status of many species, but particularly about humans. Nothing will be left to subjective opinion or guesswork.

Professionals in sex research may find our first three chapters too elementary (though sexual facts, like sexual acts, are often more pleasurable with repetition); some lay persons may find these three chapters too technical (though stimulating subject matter facilitates comprehension). In either case, the reader may certainly skip them and proceed to Chapter 4. Accepting and understanding our theory does not depend on mere facts. Our work has been conducted in the great tradition of modern science; the facts are largely superfluous.

Anatomic Types

Anatomically, we can divide all animals into the following types:

1. Reproductives. Creatures who reproduce asexually, who are incapable of experiencing sexual pleasure. This group includes the amoeba and the protozoa. (And sometimes I wonder about most Catholic women.)

1.5 Alternators. Creatures who alternate between being reproductives and sexuo-reproductives.

In her remarkable study of the lives of six sea squirts, Amora Lingaard detected primitive passion in this species which, though legless, straddles the reproductive and sexuo-reproductive rungs of the evolutionary ladder.*

2. Sexuo-Reproductives. The broad range of creatures who experience sexual feeling (or seem to), but whose sexuality is tied inextricably to reproductive activity.

■ *Full-gendered alternators* are sexuo-reproductives who go back and forth between maleness and femaleness. Hagfish and edible oysters alternate in this way; limpets develop full penises as males and re-absorb them when female.**

It has been hypothesized that the greater incidence of transvestism among men than among women indicates a throwback to alternator origins in the former. (Judstrap, Rebinka, "Taking Turns: The Biological Basis of Indecision in Man, Part I," *Reproduction Quarterly*, January–March, 1971.)

■ *Variables* are sexuo-reproductives who are neuter when young, but develop into either males or females depending on the conditions under which they are reared. Marine worms, for example, become female if allowed to develop independently, but male if they mature in contact with a female.

---

* Lingaard, Amora, *The Birth of Passion.* (New York: Impact Press, 1979). This scientist's journal reads like a suspense novel. Here is an excerpt: "4 April 1975. This morning, my research has borne fruit! The dark winter months of constant vigil, hope, exhaustion, and doubts are behind me. Moby and Tarry were in physical contact in the lower northeast corner of tank #4. At 05:09, my respirometers registered a significant increase in oxygen consumption in the vicinity of Moby and Tarry. They were panting!"

** For a thought provoking essay on the significance of limpet anatomy, see Margaret Terwilliger's "What Would Freud Have Said to a Limpet?" in F.C. Garside, ed. *Best Sex Essays of the Sixties.* (New York: Basil Books, 1970).

It has been hypothesized that the greater incidence of transsexualism among men than among women indicates a throwback to marine worm origins in the former. (Judstrap, Rebinka, "Changing: The Biological Basis of Indecision in Man. Part II," *Reproduction Quarterly,* October-December, 1971.)

My Uncle Henry (who is a Marine, but not really a worm) is quite possibly a variable. Born with a confusing genital, my grandmother slept with him until he was three, nursed him until he was four, and takes full credit for the descension of testicles and the emergence of a bona fide penis during his kindergarten year. (Figure 1-1)

Figure 1.1   There is no longer any confusion about Uncle Henry's gender.

The variable nature of female birds is discussed at length in Robert White and Robert Link's parakeet study.* As has been known for some time, removal of the functional ovary in a female bird results in her rudimentary ovary developing into a testis, and the bird becoming male. White and Link's searching psychological study traces the frantic and fearful behavior changes in six female parakeets subjected to surgical removal of their functional ovaries. All six did indeed become functional males, and seriously disturbed.

■ *Hermaphrodites,* those versatile sexuo-reproductives, are at once male and female. A tapeworm's head is male and tail female, thus bearing a striking resemblance to Phyllis Schlafly.

Disease and other influences can induce hermaphroditism among mammals, perhaps including humans. However, there is no reason to worry that your child may lose his or her sexual definition during a bout with the flu; post-gestation influences rarely affect gender.

■ *Upper Sexuo-Reproductives* have definite, constant, and separate male and female members. Practically all the species whose names are household words are in this very large group. For example, rats, dogs, crocodiles, men, pigeons, and mosquitoes. Their common denominator is lust, gratifiable through reproductive acts.

3. Sexuals. The true human is a sexual (not to be confused with asexual)—the pinnacle of evolution (among the scientific), the crown of creation (among the religious). (Figure 1.2)

Sexuals commonly engage in reproductive acts during which they experience no sexual feeling. Conversely, they may experience the most heightened sexual gratification in a non-reproductive activity. Sex and reproduction are no more closely connected in the sexuals than are defecation and breathing. But even educated people persist in believing that the sexuo-reproductive link exists in all species.**

---

* White, Robert and Robert O. Link, *Freud Is For the Birds: The Castration Complex in Female Parakeets.* (Cambridge, MA: Harvard University Press, Harvard Monograph Series, 1973).

** Fitemaster, Genevieve, Jocelyn Meyeravend, and Valerie Agnes Trimmer, "The Sexuo-Reproductive Myth," *Journal of Sexual Mythology,* vol. 6, no. 3, 1976.

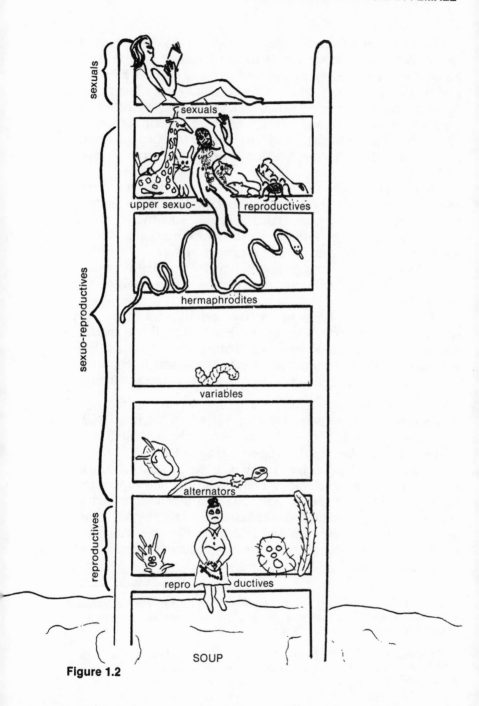

Figure 1.2

It is a clear case of majority rule. Because the sexuo-reproductives outnumber both the reproductives and the sexuals, they have effectively brainwashed the entire animal kingdom into believing that sex and reproduction are inextricably connected.

There is such confusion on this issue that, for example, a typical "sex education" course for young women may never mention words like "orgasm," "passion," or "fulfillment," but be comprised entirely of dry, technical information about contraception, pregnancy, menstruation, and the anatomy of reproductive organs. This makes about as much sense as dissecting a fetal pig in a food preparation class.

One gay male lab technician who worked for me briefly claimed that he was a sexual, not a sexuo-reproductive, since there was no chance of his impregnating any of his boyfriends.

His objection is absurd. Any man who produces sperm and deposits it in orifices is a sexuo-reproductive. The impulse to thrust one's organ into a hole—whether it be a pig's vagina, an old mitten, an orange juice can, a man's anus, a woman's mouth, or a VW exhaust pipe—and ejaculate is proof of nature's sexuo-reproductive scheme. A few sperm find their way into fertile vaginas, just as a few acorns fall on fertile ground and produce mighty oaks. It is senseless to quibble about where the rest of the sperm and acorns are diverted.

In Figure 1.3, a chart of reproductive types, you will note that, though outranked by woman, man does achieve parity with his best friend, the dog.

Sexual Organs: A Specialty

■ *"Making Do."* Evolutionists determine the evolutionary standing of species largely on the basis of their anatomic complexity. Lack of specialization of body parts characterizes lower (less-evolved) animals.

For example, the male octopus must stoop to employing one of his several arms as a penis, merely handing over sperm to his mate at breeding time. This is a remarkable fact, considering that even

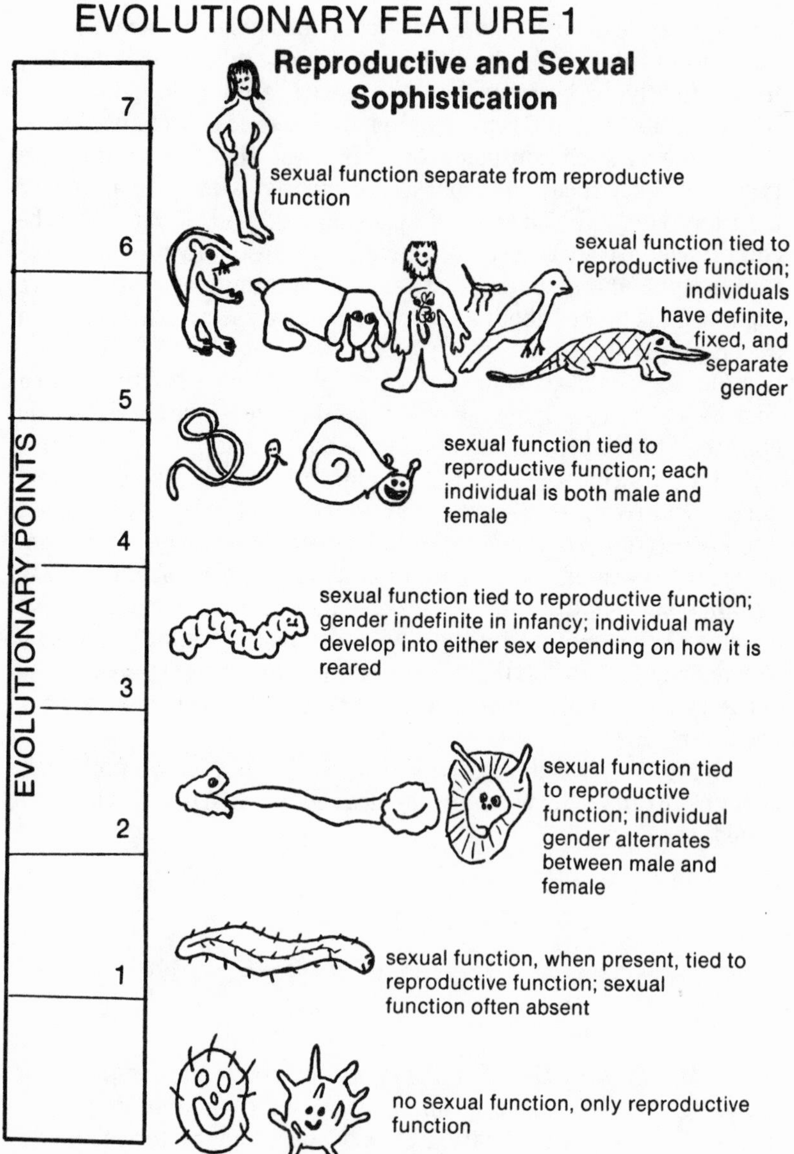

EVOLUTIONARY FEATURE 1

Reproductive and Sexual Sophistication

EVOLUTIONARY POINTS

7

sexual function separate from reproductive function

6

sexual function tied to reproductive function; individuals have definite, fixed, and separate gender

5

sexual function tied to reproductive function; each individual is both male and female

4

sexual function tied to reproductive function; gender indefinite in infancy; individual may develop into either sex depending on how it is reared

3

sexual function tied to reproductive function; individual gender alternates between male and female

2

1

sexual function, when present, tied to reproductive function; sexual function often absent

no sexual function, only reproductive function

Figure 1.3   In our study, animals can earn "Evolutionary Points" (EP's) on the basis of how they compare with other creatures on evolutionary features. At the close of Chapter 3 we will present a cumulative table of EP's summarizing all we have learned about relative evolutionary status among the myriad members of the animal kingdom.

many insects have penises. However, octopi have eight limbs and insects have only six, so the degree of hardship is not really comparable.

Also lacking a penis, the male argonaut (not the type in the legends, but the type rather like a squid in a shell) makes ingenious use of one of his legs. The argonaut is ordinarily only about half an inch long, but during breeding season one of the male's eight tiny legs becomes enormous—approximately five inches long—and then detaches itself from its body to go searching for a female to give sperm to.*

Raulie Sandiel and Ginga Zakett, former research scientists at the Center, performed some preliminary research on the argonaut, manipulating the laboratory environment so that there were always several male argonauts in breeding season. The research was promising; if other scientists had been in charge, we might know a great deal more about argonaut sexuo-reproduction now than we do.

However, one day several months into the research program, I made an unannounced visit to Sandiel and Zakett's laboratory, and to my horror found both scientists gratifying their own wanton desires with the legs of breeding argonauts. Sandiel and Zakett were given five minutes to dry, put on their clothes, and be off the premises. No trustworthy researcher has been found to finish the project.

Only slightly less sensational than the argonaut are some of the creatures who were displayed in the "Reproductive Oddities" collection of the now defunct Museum of Zoological Reproduction in Boston: dogfish who mate with their fins; spiders who accomplish coitus with bulbs on their heads; jellyfish who reproduce via fellatio; leeches who shoot each other with arrows; lizards and snakes with two penises each; oppossums with forked penises, and cats with barbed ones.

Unfortunately, this remarkable museum was closed on 18 November 1981 by the B.P.D. Vice Squad when it was found to be a front for a chimpanzee prostitution ring.

---

* Although there are many primitive aspects of the male beast human, as we shall see, at least the female human does not have to contend with enormous, prowling, disembodied penises. The beast human has unquestionably out-evolved the argonaut in this regard.

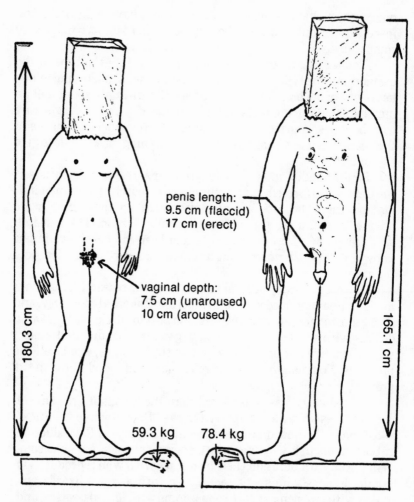

penis length:
9.5 cm (flaccid)
17 cm (erect)

vaginal depth:
7.5 cm (unaroused)
10 cm (aroused)

180.3 cm

165.1 cm

59.3 kg   78.4 kg

Figure 1.4   Of the 217 applicants for the position of Typical Specimen, 11 persons had remarkably large or small genitals. If this sample is representative of the populace, 5% of our population must suffer from the distressing malady of genital mismatch. Our 11 exceptional applicants founded a support group for persons with extreme sized genitals, which provides crisis counseling and matchmaking services for distressed clients. Women with aroused vaginal sizes under 8 cm. or over 12 cm., and men with aroused penis lengths of under 14 cm. or over 20 cm. are eligible for service. To start a chapter in your area, send your name, address, and genital size to BIG and small/Box 0009/Seattle, WA 98111.

It is probable that the prevalence of sadism in man indicates a hereditary kinship with the leech. (Coffman, Flory, "The Martyrdom of Saint Sebastian: Was It A Gangbang?" chapter six from *Saints as Sinners,* Vulcan Press, New York, 1981.)

It has been hypothesized that the often decided preference for fellatio rather than vaginal intercourse among men indicates an ancestral kinship with the jellyfish. (Coalman, Kay Bea, "The Primitive Origins of Fellatio as Evidenced in Several Modern Species," *Genitalia,* vol. 4, no. 1, 1976.)

Human Anatomy. We are all familiar with the basic anatomical features of *Homo veridis* and *Homo bestias,* but a detailed examination is in order to see how their anatomies fit into the total evolutionary scheme.

A group of five M.D.'s performed extensive physical examinations and recorded detailed histories on 217 men and women who applied to our study as physically normal specimens of their kind. Lloyd Harbinger, 31, and Joyce Shannonwalter, 33, were ranked as the most representative physical examples of their sexes. (Figure 1.4)

Lloyd's and Joyce's bodies are homologous in most respects. It is only upon investigating the degree of complexity and intricacy of the reproductive and sexual equipment that the differences are absolutely striking.

Lloyd has no complicated internal network of reproductive organs. It was verified by surgical procedure that he has no *simple* internal reproductive organs either. By contrast, Joyce has inside her body ovaries, Fallopian tubes, and a marvelous organ called a uterus in which she gestated her two children. This organ is so delicately designed that it will function optimally only about one or two more times, which indicates that Joyce, as a typical human female, is designed to have extremely limited procreative duties during her lifetime. These ovaries and tubes and this uterus are all solely reproductive in nature.

Also inside, leading to the outside, Joyce has a urethra, which is exclusively excretory. On the outside she has a delightful little

EVOLUTIONARY FEATURE 2

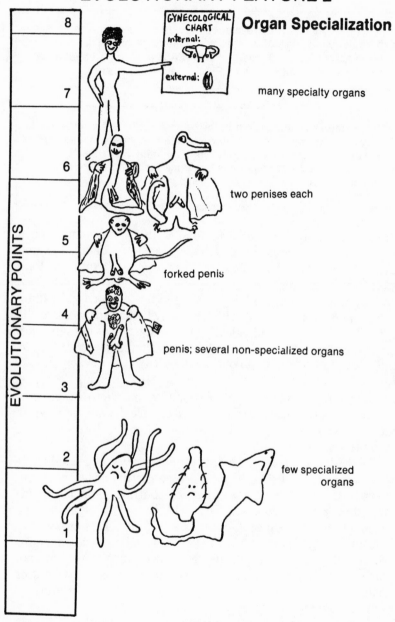

Organic Specialization

Figure 1.5

clitoris, which is exclusively sexual in function. Her vagina is primarily a reproductive organ, but Joyce attests to its having some sexual significance as well.*

On Lloyd we found a penis and a urethra, both of which are elimino-sexuo-reproductive, and two testes, which are sexuo-reproductive. This accounts for all of it. As Figure 1.5 indicates, Lloyd's primitive equipment places him slightly below the opossum on this evolutionary feature.

A Tribute

A pause to pay tribute to one of the real pioneers in the study of human reproductive anatomy is in order. Although I can nowhere in Sigmund Freud's writings find the exact phrase "Anatomy is Destiny" which is so often attributed to him, his message to that effect is certainly clear enough, and we cannot fault the man for an inability to turn a catchy phrase. One of Freud's aims was to reconcile one of the sexes to its destiny as baby maker and establish that the other sex is, by comparison, quite free from procreative concerns.

In this chapter, we have begun to see the truth in Freud's theory, and we will see additional evidence in the pages to come. To have had the entire theory correct except for one minor detail—the question of which of the sexes is naturally, anatomically destined for the task of reproduction, and which of the sexes is free from it to pursue higher endeavors—marks Freud as a researcher who was both rarely insightful and far ahead of his time.

---

* This claim was reiterated by some other heterosexual females who worked in our program, but was contradicted by most of the lesbians we studied. Thus, we believe the purported sexual significance is purely psychological.

Summary

Man is a *sexuo-reproductive*; woman is a *sexual*. Like many lower animals, man has no specific sexual organs, but must use non-sexual body parts to do "double duty" as sex organs. His anatomical destiny is procreation. Woman's intricate sexual system is independent of her reproductive system. The destiny of her anatomy appears to be up to her.

chapter 2

The Naked Physiological Facts

We have seen how animal sexuo-reproductive equipment is built; let's look at how it works. As we do so, we will see additional evidence of the long evolutionary struggle to emancipate sexuality from reproduction.

Reproductive Seasons

puberty/spring

Non-human beasts. Puberty is that exciting period of ripening of the animal body during which hormones make the animal's reproductive gear functional. My research team naturally wondered whether most animals ripen sexually at the same time as they ripen reproductively. That is, does a wombat feel passion with its first erection? At what time of life is the average Gila monster first capable of real desire? Do erotic dreams accompany the first nocturnal emissions of weasels?

To our amazement, we found no answers to these vital questions in the literature. The complete dearth of available scientific information about sexual awakening in animals was scandalous. We saw our duty and we did it.

We studied two Bactrian camels (Royal and Plebia), two wombats (Robert and Megan), two Gila monsters (Peter and Jackie), two weasels (Gary and Kathy), and two three-toed sloths (Steve and Sally). All the creatures were studied before, during, and after the

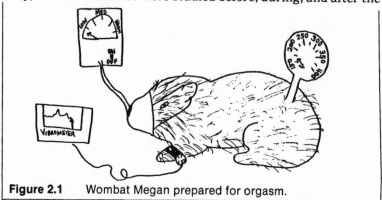

Figure 2.1   Wombat Megan prepared for orgasm.

puberal age range of their particular species. We collected egg/ sperm samples from each species to confirm the arrival of puberty. To determine the presence of orgasm or peak sexual arousal, we used thermometers, vibrometers, respirometers, and subjective judgment. (Figure 2.1)

There was remarkable uniformity of sexual and reproductive achievement among all five species. Let's look at Royal the camel as an example. During his pre-pubescent months in our experimental play yard, researcher Viola Maynard made determined efforts to arouse him sexually.

Viola's first step was to fasten a huge poster on the wall over Royal's bed of straw. The poster depicted a voluptuous young woman wearing only a turban, strolling in the desert. The caption under the picture read, "I'd walk a mile for a camel." The poster failed to evoke sexual interest in Royal, so Viola next tried less subtle tactics.

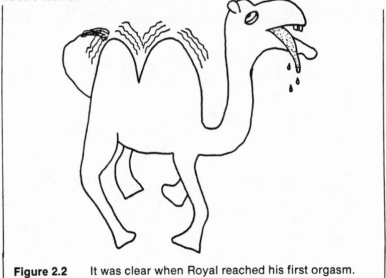

Figure 2.2   It was clear when Royal reached his first orgasm.

She read him pornographic books about lewd camels performing every sexual feat that the species is capable of. She showed him movies of camel orgies. Thinking that perhaps Royal was gay, she introduced pictures of handsome male camels with splendid erect penises. These techniques also failed to elicit sexual interest.

About two months later, in April, Royal was back in his play yard again, this time with our other Bactrian, Plebia. He was chewing some imaginary food, as is his custom. When Plebia brushed up against him on her way to a gorse bush, both of Royal's humps trembled, his tongue protruded momentarily, his eyeballs rolled up under his lids, and his tail stiffened. Royal had achieved his first orgasm. Viola hurriedly gathered up a sample of the sticky liquid which Royal's penis had emitted during the seizure. It contained sperm, the first recorded for Royal. (Figure 2.2)

For all five species that we studied, orgasm (or peak sexual arousal) and ejaculation/ovulation became possible at the same time; and the fertilizing (reproductive) act of ejaculation or fertile coitus constituted the orgasm or sexual expression. Only the orgasmic symptoms showed any variety. (Our weasel Gary's first orgasmic shriek terrified the laboratory staff. Steve the sloth swooned and fell eight feet from his perch onto a concrete floor after his first climax.) (Figure 2.3)

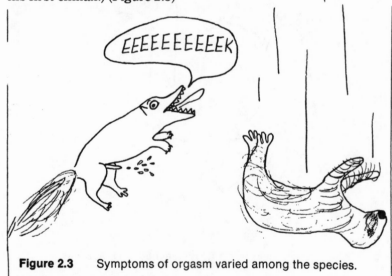

Figure 2.3   Symptoms of orgasm varied among the species.

Beast humans. Like the camel, wombat, Gila monster, three-toed sloth, and weasel, the beast human achieves sexual functioning with reproductive functioning—at puberty.

There are a few contradictory opinions on this point. Some authorities, including Kinsey, have stated that complete orgasm is possible for the beast human from birth; that semen appears first at puberty and sperm even later; and that ejaculation and orgasm can occur independently in the adult male. All of my own findings (in direct field work, and in extensive interviews of subjects injected with sodium pentathol) contradict these views. I can only conclude from this discrepancy that these authorities are deliberately perpetrating yet another of the sexual myths this species is famous for fabricating, or that they are being misled by rumor-mongers, or that they have information about the miniscule portion of the male population that is true human and could be presumed to be capable of these feats. I can state with certainty that any pre-ejaculatory boy who is believed to have experienced orgasm is either faking it (another ancient ploy of this species) or is one of the very small number of true human males.

There is erective ability prior to puberty, which, incidentally, enables the boy to rape even before he can impregnate. This erective capability might mislead some persons into believing there are accompanying orgasmic episodes. Intercourse may certainly occur, but nothing comes of it; or, at least, I can state unequivocally that I have never had intercourse with a pre-pubescent boy who came, nor have I ever known anyone who has. (Figure 2.4)

We asked our typical male human specimen, Lloyd Harbinger, whether he had experienced orgasm or ejaculation first. He answered, "That's like asking me whether I learned to pee or piss first. What's the difference?" We were never able to explain the difference to Lloyd, but his response clearly indicates that the average beast human does not distinguish between orgasm and ejaculation.

Figure 2.4   The mouse is one of only two species in the animal kingdom known to commit rape. (Steinback, Jan, *Of Mouse and Man,* Provocative Press, New York, 1962.)

As you will see in Figure 2.5, the beast human does no worse than any other beast when ranked on this evolutionary factor.

EVOLUTIONARY FEATURE 3
Correlation Between Sexuality and Puberty

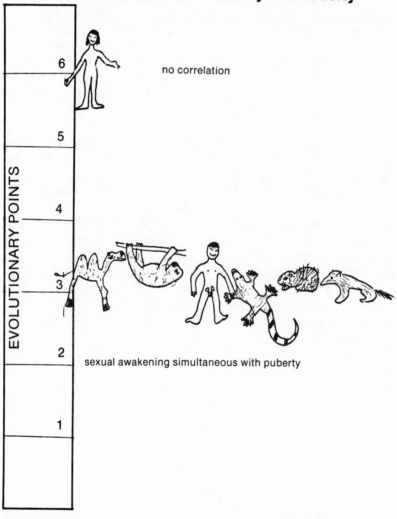

Figure 2.5

True humans. At puberty, the true human ripens her first eggs, and is thus capable of reproducing. It becomes perfectly possible (in fact, more probable than the unfortunate young girl may at first perceive) for the post-puberal female true human to conceive, carry, and deliver young without the slightest tinge of concomitant sexual pleasure. The reproductive and sexual functions are entirely independent.

The true human may coincidentally become orgasmic at puberty, or she may become orgasmic long after puberty, or never at all. We asked our typical human female specimen, Joyce Shannonwalter, whether she had experienced ovulation or orgasm first. She had no difficulty in distinguishing the two; she first ovulated at age 13 and had her first orgasm at age 23. A full ten years separated her initiation into reproductive capacity from her initiation into sexual capacity.

The true human may be orgasmic long before puberty. Female infants as young as four months of age have been observed in orgasm. My own research indicates that girl babies are sometimes multiply orgasmic if they are being rocked at the same time they are feeding.* (These are breast-fed babies; bottle-fed infants are rarely orgasmic before 17 months of age.)

The infant orgasm often is accompanied by urinating, momentary cessation of sucking, and a pleasant little squeal. Orgasmic occurrences during infancy are sometimes the first positive indication that the female is definitely of the true human species. Of course, there is no cause for concern if a female infant is not orgasmic, since a good many true human females never achieve orgasm at any point in life.

coitus/summer

Non-human beasts. Being sexuo-reproductives, non-human beasts seek coitus only when they are fertile.** For example, I can't get a

---

* Hermen, Pegasus, "The Importance of Early Clitoral Discovery in Rearing Sexually Competent Girls," *Journal of Pediatric Sexual Dysfunction*, vol. 2, no. 2, 1976.

** An occasional infertile baboon will allow penetration rather than endure some other abuse. We see this kind of behavior in our own species as well, and certainly such coital episodes do not have sexual, i.e. pleasurable, content. The truly sexual encounters of female baboons are fertile ones.

lick of work out of my faithful farm horse Amanda when she is in heat. But when her heat passes, she settles contentedly back into her job, not even looking at Tobias, the stallion in the next pasture, until her next heat. And once Tobias exhausts his sperm supply, he falls in a sleepy heap.

There is a magnificent exception to this sexuo-reproductive fact. As my house ape, a chimpanzee named Ruthie, has demonstrated countless times with her small, battery-operated vibrator, female anthropoid apes sometimes enjoy coitus when they are not fertile. Ruthie's electric dildo gets much more frequent use when she is fertile, but the fact that she does take pleasure in coitus when she cannot conceive sets her and her ape friends apart from other sexuo-reproductive species. (Figure 2.6)

Figure 2.6

Beast humans. Typical male human Lloyd exemplifies the situation of the beast human. Time and time again, we observed him in the lab. His sexual interest, like Tobias the stallion's, was extinguished whenever his sperm supply was depleted.

True humans. Ovulation is neither prompted nor curtailed by sexual interest in women. On the contrary, women, left to their natural inclinations, will desire sexual activity and orgasm as intensely when incapable of conception as they will in times of fertility. Paradoxically, a majority of female humans experience their greatest sexual desire during and close to the menstrual period, the time when they are least likely to conceive; and many report a marked increase in sexual desire during pregnancy, another inconceivable time. This might indicate a correlation—a reverse one—between sex and reproduction in true humans. However, my own belief is that the preference for sex during infertile periods is psychological rather than physiological. Only heterosexual women who are madly in love are ordinarily stimulated by the thought of reproducing, and among that group, fertile times do become sexual. Women who have their wits about them become less responsive—often temporarily frigid—at the thought of pregnancy.

On this evolutionary feature, the true human wins, the anthropoid ape places, and the baboon shows. The beast human finishes out of the money. (Figure 2.7)

A Postscript to Catholics. Though the Pope may be infallible, he is clearly susceptible to confusion. In his celebrated 1968 encyclical *Humanae Vitae,* Pope Paul VI bases his conclusions about the morality of contraception on the purported fact that sexual arousal is an integral part of the reproductive act and urge, and that sexual desire is dependent on reproductive behavior for its very existence. But since no such association exists between sex and reproduction in true humans, the encyclical is not applicable to most women.

Of course, some percentage of Catholic women are bound to be beast humans. The Pope might have been guilty only of careless semantics rather than actual confusion. He might simply have neglected to specify which "humanae" he was addressing. I would suggest that the Vatican change the title of the document to *Humanae Bestiae Vitae.* This would spare the majority of Catholic women a great deal of needless soul-searching and distress when considering the issue of contraception.

EVOLUTIONARY FEATURE 4
Fertility of Coital Episodes

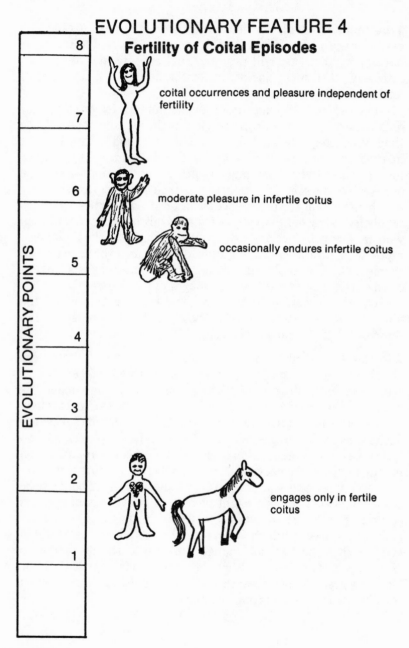

EVOLUTIONARY POINTS

8

7   coital occurrences and pleasure independent of
    fertility

6   moderate pleasure in infertile coitus

5   occasionally endures infertile coitus

4

3

2   engages only in fertile
    coitus

1

Figure 2.7

the climacteric/fall

Non-human beasts. Very little primary research has been performed in the area of menopause, or the climacteric, in non-human species. Informal observation of my old dog Muffin, and my past pets Mox (a dog), Murphy, Miss O'Toole, Tufftetta Jean (cats), and Pogo (a raccoon) indicates that when they stopped siring or bearing litters, they stopped lusting as well. This is characteristic of sexuo-reproductive beasts.

Beast humans. The age at which beast humans reach their climacteric is difficult to estimate. We interviewed 37 men ranging in age from 63 to 96, and not one of them reported the slightest diminution in sexuo-reproductive functioning. All refused sperm counts; all said they were bachelors or widowers, so we could not talk with their wives.

One subject volunteered that he plays Senior Bingo twice a week with his "brothers" at the Temple of the Protective Order of the Loyal Moose. He reports that the men get all worked up playing Bingo, and at about midnight go out in a pack to a brothel two blocks away.

It so happens that I have a dear personal friend who works at this very brothel. She has confided in me that not a single one of the Bingo-playing Mooses has ever removed more than his overcoat and hat in her room, and that the most vigorous activity in which she has engaged with any of them has been a game of checkers. Her favorite Moose is a 79-year-old homosexual who has never come out of the closet. For him, she keeps a stack of pictures of naked young men to look at while he sits contentedly in her rocking chair, stroking his limp "Tiger."

Normally the Mooses stay about forty minutes, smudge a little lipstick on their necks and ears, tangle their hair, pull their shirttails part way out of their pants, unzip their flies about halfway, and charge out the door with their brethren, all chuckling and snorting, to the tavern across the street.

The logical conclusion to draw is that—at whatever age—sexual desire subsides at the same rate and at the same time as reproductive capability in men.

As you will see in Figure 2.8, the beast human ranks with some very companionable species on this evolutionary feature.

True humans. We interviewed 29 post-menopausal women, one of whom was Kitte van Gelder, Joyce Shannonwalter's mother. All of

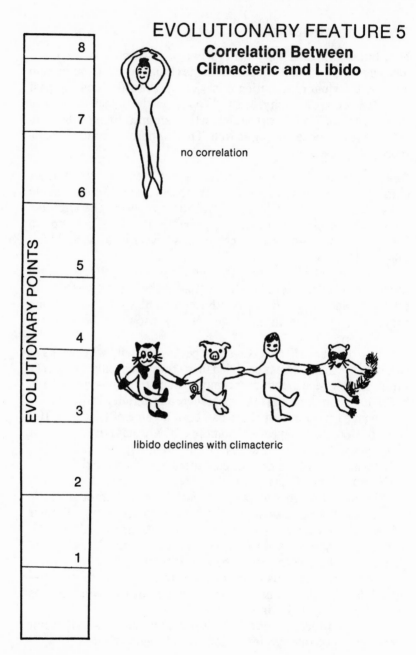

EVOLUTIONARY FEATURE 5
Correlation Between
Climacteric and Libido

no correlation

libido declines with climacteric

EVOLUTIONARY POINTS

Figure 2.8

these women ceased ovulating between the ages of 43 and 56. Eighteen experienced no change in sexual desire or capacity, and eleven noticed an increase.*

necrotica/winter

Until recently, I was willing to rest my case at the grave. My own view of heaven was that death equalized all species; that there was no evolutionary status in the hereafter; that snails, goats, and all the rest of us reached a final harmony without regard to evolutionary standing.

However, preliminary data from the Sexuo-Psychic Research Center in Los Angeles suggest otherwise. The Research Center has grown out of a thesis project which Tara Hinton undertook in the fall of 1954 to fulfill the requirements for a Ph.D. in Sexology from Paragon College.

Tara chose the following thesis topic: "Establishing a Correlation Between Sexual Fulfillment on Earth and Sexual Fulfillment in Paradise." (Tara is Roman Catholic. The choice of her participating subjects, the nature of her heaven, and other details of her research reflect a Roman Catholic bias.) She recruited 250 married, heterosexually active persons between the ages of 20 and 76, 125 of each sex. From 1954 through 1956 she documented sexual histories on each of them, including their fantasies, their frustrations, and their transgressions. All 250 subjects must die before Tara's dissertation can be completed. She hopes that of the 250 total, at least 25 men and 25 women will make it to heaven and then—as they have promised to do—return to her in seances to describe their sex lives in Paradise.

To date, 39 women and 47 men in the research pool have died. Nineteen of the women and six of the men have arrived in heaven and reported back to Tara. A few representative comments from their reports follow.

---

* Unfortunately, the increased desire led to increased sexual frustration for seven of these women because the only desire their husbands had was for backgammon or poker. But on the bright side, the increased libido was not wasted on the other four women, who were lesbians.

Gerald O.: I have but the dimmest recollection of what sexual desire was like. Being a purely physical drive, it is alien to me in my spiritual state.

Jocelyn P.: I just arrived two days ago, and I feel the way I did when I went to camp the summer after second grade. I've looked forward to it for so long, but I am so lonely. Charles didn't make it here, and though he was not a very loving husband on earth, I had always dreamed of our perfect marriage in eternity. My dear cocker spaniel, Toby, is not here either, good though he always was. Only humans are allowed in.

Joel M.: Though I was tempted by other women during my life on earth, I was always faithful to Mabel. Here in heaven I no longer defile my beloved Mabel, because I am free of the Satanic lust for sexual intercourse which plagued me on earth. I always dreamed of this for Mabel, and yet she seems less pleased with me now.

Mary Mc.: On earth Maria L. and I were very good friends. But here in heaven we have learned the mutual achievement of divine ecstasy.

The implications of Hinton's research are clear. When the physical body is gone, and with it the ability to reproduce, the sex urge completely disappears for the beast human. Sexual desire lives eternal for the true human.

Hormonal/Cortical Dominance

Breeding behavior is governed by two tyrants: the *cerebral cortex* and the *hormones*. These two tyrants vie for dominance, and whichever tyrant is the stronger in a particular species dominates the breeding behavior of that species.

Our primary interest lies with the *horticals* and the *corticals*. The *horticals* include most of the primates (e.g., chimpanzees, beast humans, gorillas). A few authorities claim the power of the hormone tyrant and the cortex tyrant to be equal in this group, but my own feeling is that the chimpanzee/beast human susceptibility to hormone therapy and the degree of malfunction due to gonadal loss both indicate that the hormone tyrant—without a doubt—still has the upper hand.*

Certainly, brain surgery has done far less to correct sexual disturbances in beast humans and chimpanzees than have hormone shots.

The true human is the only species in whom the cortical tyrant reigns supreme over the hormonal tyrant in the sexual sphere. She comprises the *corticals*. In fact, the hormone tyrant is completely absent from her sexual sphere. Its dominion is reproduction, and only that dominion suffers if gonads, the hormonal-reproductive stronghold, are removed. (Figure 2.9)

Cerebro-Psychic/Neuro-Spinal Participation in Executing the Sexual Will

Although the cortex and the hormones vie for sexuo-reproductive dominance, additional systems are necessary to execute** sexual behavior, or the sexual will. Executors of the sexual will include the circulatory system, the respiratory system, the musculature, the infracerebral nervous system (spinal cord), and the brain. It is in the relative participation of the last two executors mentioned—the spinal cord and the brain—that we find signifi-

---

* See sources listed below:

1. Trimmer, Valerie Agnes, "The Cortical-Hormonal Standoff," *Hormone*, vol. 6, no. 1, 1975.
2. Lenoir, Suzette, "La Signification de L'Ecorce dans L'Acte Sexuel," *Sexe Au'jourd'hui*, Mai, 1973.
3. Durand, Madeleine et Suzette Lenoir, "L'Égalité des Deux Tyrans," *Journal de l'Hormone*, vol. 42, no. 6, 1975.
4. Lenoir, Suzette, "Le Traitement par les Hormones de Deux Grands Singes: l'Homme et le Chimpanze," *Therapie Revue*, Fev. 1972.
5. Lenoir, Suzette and Valerie Agnes Trimmer, "The Brief Details of the Sex Lives of Seven Young Men Devoid of Their Testicles," *Sexuo-Reproductive Yearbook*, 1975.

** In the sense of "carry out," not "punish by killing," although the latter sometimes occurs as well.

EVOLUTIONARY FEATURE 6
Cortical vs. Hormonal Dominance of Sexuality

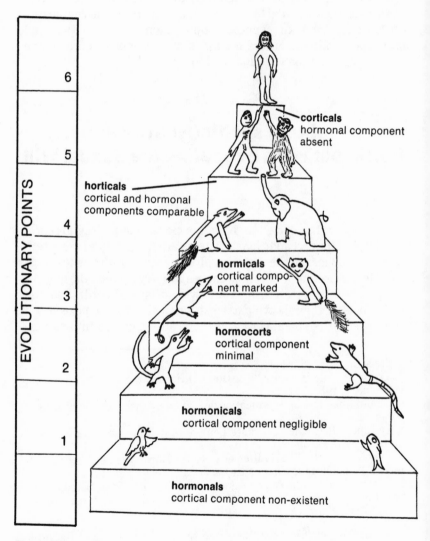

Figure 2.9

cant indication of evolutionary status.

Evidence in the literature strongly suggests that erections and emissions of semen in men depend upon nervous impulses from the spinal column and may occur with no contribution whatsoever from the brain. (Lloyd refused to allow us to confirm this fact because he was afraid we would not be able to reconnect his spinal cord to his brain after the experiment.) However, it is believed that men with spinal cords intact but severed from the brain engage in coitus significantly less frequently than do men with brains and spinal cords connected. Thus, some cerebral contribution in some coital episodes must be acknowledged. Also, totally brainless men with intact spinal cords are believed incapable of coital connection, so again, some credit for cerebral involvement must be allowed.

Josef Lemur and Thomas Tarsier were decapitated in an automobile accident in June 1980. Although recovering satisfactorily after restorative surgery, both men confess that they are less sexually active than they were prior to the accident. (Lipton, Tracy P., "Re-Capitation: the Surgical Procedure Bringing New Hope to People Who Lose Their Heads," *Kentucky Surgery Journal,* December 1981.)

We did not wish to impose upon typical specimen Joyce for confirmation of some facts. But it is known that orgasms in women are wholly cerebro-psychic dependent. All the spinal stimulation in the world cannot ignite one, nor can the totality of infra-cerebral impulses suppress one. However, because the neurological system is believed to be necessary to help teach orgasmic response, we must debit for some spinal participation.*

Because of the dearth of research in this area on any species other than the two human ones, I made an effort to perform experiments on several species myself. However, specimens kept dying under the anesthesia or succumbing to secondary infections following neural surgery, so no data were obtainable. We lost, in all, 21 rats (14 female, 7 male), 3 giraffes (2 female, 1 male), 18 skunks (11 female, 7 male), 9 porcupines (3 female, 6 male), 1 lobster (sex

---

* Lildevahl, Virginia and Roberta Nell Sandbloom, "Possible Culpability of the Spine in Seven Cases of Orgasmic Dysfunction," *Cord,* vol. 4, no. 3, 1977.

undetermined), and 2 geoducks (a lesbian couple). One additional skunk survived, but has remained in a coma, and has thus been unable to provide information.* I am, therefore, unable to supply my readers with specific data at that time. Figure 2.10 is based upon preliminary estimates and may have to be revised in light of future research.

Complexity of Response

The relative complexity of a species' sex response appears to be correlated with evolutionary ranking. Interestingly, sex research pioneers Masters and Johnson found the true human's sex response cycle to be extremely varied and complex, the beast human's predictable and simple. My own findings in Figure 2.11 concur with theirs.

As you can see, the beast human travels the same, well-worn, unswerving path every time he ascends Mt. Orgasm. His speedy and graceless descent is equally predictable. The true human, by contrast, rarely travels the same path twice, and her network of trails is so intricate and mysterious that only a few of the better known landmarks and main trails could be included in our figure.

Research material on other species is almost totally lacking, but I have gathered some data on a few animals. To chart their response cycles, I needed objective, measurable physiological events, such as sex flush, hyperventilation, and muscle tension. These events were difficult for me to detect in the dogs, rats, ground squirrels, guppies, and toads that I studied because the instrumentation interfered with their sexuo-reproductive interest and performance. However, sex flush has for the first time been recorded among a few of these creatures (2 Pomeranians and 4 rats) who were shaved for experimental purposes.

---

* The blood of these beasts is upon those who have turned down my grant proposals. Lack of sufficient funding has forced me to use rather crude techniques and outdated equipment for many of my experiments. This has produced inexact results and—as in the present case—tragedy.

EVOLUTIONARY FEATURE 7
Primary Executors of the Sexual Will

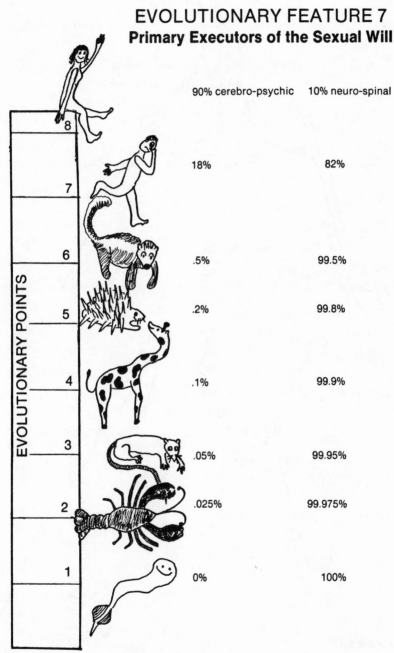

90% cerebro-psychic   10% neuro-spinal

Point	cerebro-psychic	neuro-spinal
8	90%	10%
7	18%	82%
6	.5%	99.5%
5	.2%	99.8%
4	.1%	99.9%
3	.05%	99.95%
2	.025%	99.975%
1	0%	100%

EVOLUTIONARY POINTS

Figure 2.10

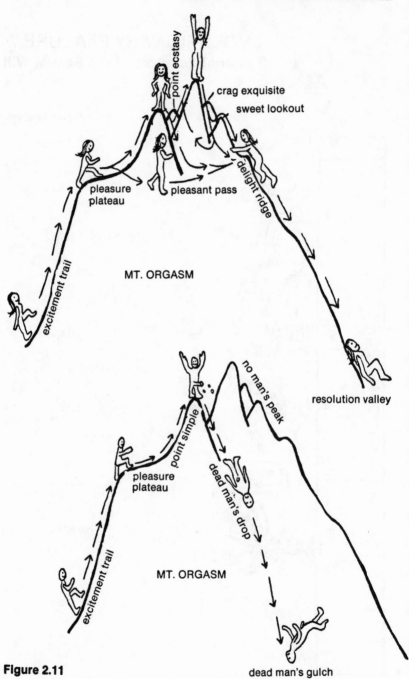

point ecstasy

crag exquisite

sweet lookout

pleasure plateau

pleasant pass

delight ridge

excitement trail

MT. ORGASM

resolution valley

point simple

no man's peak

pleasure plateau

dead man's drop

excitement trail

MT. ORGASM

dead man's gulch

Figure 2.11

My experiments revealed little variation from cycle to cycle or even from beast to beast among these animals, so I have depicted the response cycles of all five species in a single figure. (Figure 2.12)

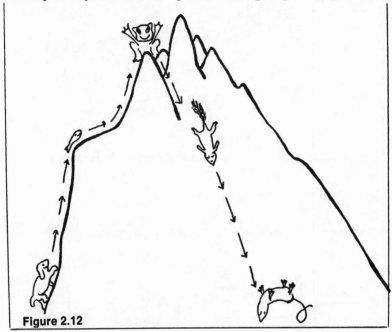

Figure 2.12

The similarity between the basic beast cycle and the beast human cycle is striking. It is, of course, possible that there is greater complexity and variation in the basic beast cycle than I was able to detect with my techniques, but no one can doubt the authenticity of the beast human cycle, backed up by eleven years of painstaking research by Masters and Johnson. Thus, further study in this area could hardly be hoped to be favorable to the beast human.

Though beast human response never varied with respect to orgasmic intensity or complexity, there was some variation in orgasmic duration. This slight evolutionary edge is reflected in Figure 2.13.

Although the scientific facts in Chapters 1 and 2 are sufficient to establish the evolutionary discrepancy between true humans and beast humans, thoroughness demands one more chapter of scientific evidence.

EVOLUTIONARY FEATURE 8
Sexual Response Cycles

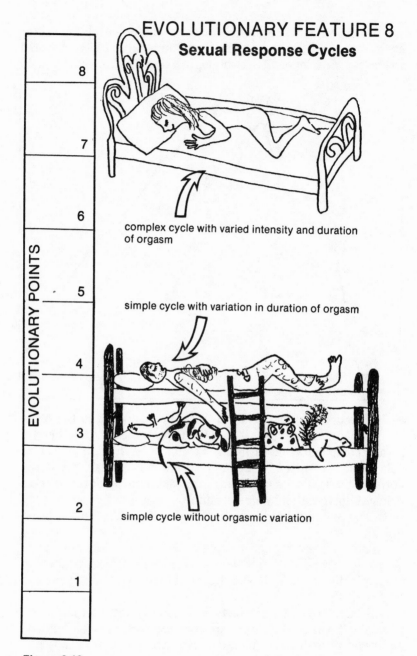

complex cycle with varied intensity and duration of orgasm

simple cycle with variation in duration of orgasm

simple cycle without orgasmic variation

EVOLUTIONARY POINTS

Figure 2.13

Summary

Like many simple animals, man is "in season," or reproductively capable, almost all of his life. His sexual functioning, like the gorilla's, is controlled largely by hormones. A sort of spinal "knee jerk" response enables him to accomplish orgasm; his simple, predictable sexual response cycle is comparable to that of a squirrel. Sexuality in woman is largely cerebral, and her intricate sexual response cycle defies exact scientific description.

chapter 3

Statistics Don't Lie

Statistics add respectability to any scientific theory, and I am proud to have a generous supply of them for mine. Some of my critics may take issue with my opinions, but can they argue with numbers?

Number of Gametes Produced

By anyone's standards, there is an unmistakable correlation between relatively large numbers of gametes (eggs and sperm) being produced and low evolutionary status. (Figure 3.1)

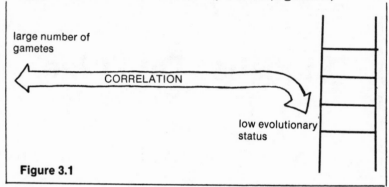

Figure 3.1

Beast humans. We asked Lloyd to collect sperm from six different masturbating sessions. We measured the volume of each batch of ejaculate, and (with the help of 48 Kelly Girls equipped with tiny tweezers) counted the number of sperm each vial contained. Our findings appear in Figure 3.2. To arrive at a lifetime sperm production figure, Lloyd suggested we use ten ejaculations per week for 70 years as a conservative base estimate. We pared that figure to one quarter, which resulted in a lifetime sperm production figure of 8,320,000,000,000,000 for the average beast human.

True humans. In consultation with Joyce, we projected her lifetime gamete (egg) production to be approximately 400. This estimate results in a disparity of 8,319,999,999,999,600 between gametes produced by the average male beast human and the average female true human. I am glad that I am not one of those who believes the two types are members of the same species. I wouldn't be able to sleep nights trying to rationalize this disparity.

Some people will undoubtedly argue that, because of the different natures of sperm and eggs, there must be many more of the former than the latter. But what then can they say about my little oyster, Marina, who last summer alone produced 500 million eggs? And what about my two experimental houseflies, Richard and Annie, who produced approximately one quintillion (1,000, 000,000,000,000,000) gametes each during the six months they were with us? Yes, Richard and Annie, mates and members of the same species, produced approximately the same number of eggs as sperm.

Even if we allow the male beast human a generous 90% discount factor to compensate for his lack of a protective internal sanctuary for his gametes, the disparity between true human female and beast human male gamete production is so great that its evolutionary significance cannot be ignored. You may compare gamete counts for a number of randomly selected species in Figure 3.3.

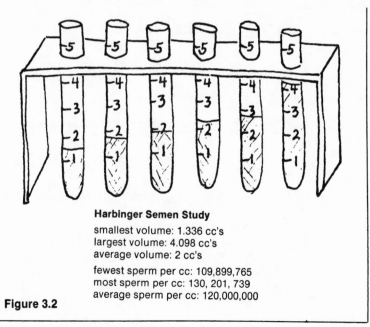

Harbinger Semen Study

smallest volume: 1.336 cc's
largest volume: 4.098 cc's
average volume: 2 cc's

fewest sperm per cc: 109,899,765
most sperm per cc: 130, 201, 739
average sperm per cc: 120,000,000

Figure 3.2

EVOLUTIONARY FEATURE 9
Number of Gametes Produced

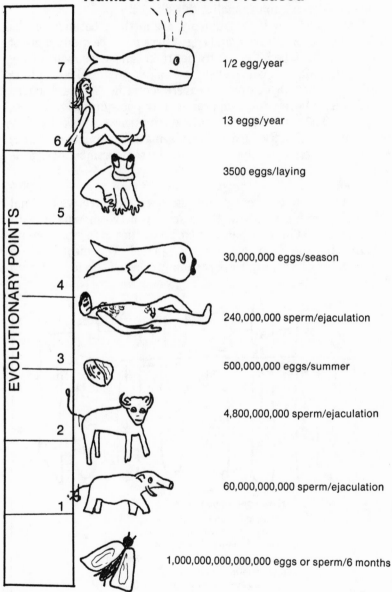

7 — 1/2 egg/year

13 eggs/year

6 — 3500 eggs/laying

5 — 30,000,000 eggs/season

4 — 240,000,000 sperm/ejaculation

3 — 500,000,000 eggs/summer

4,800,000,000 sperm/ejaculation

2 — 60,000,000,000 sperm/ejaculation

1 — 1,000,000,000,000,000 eggs or sperm/6 months

EVOLUTIONARY POINTS

Figure 3.3

Age at Reproductive Maturity

One scientific rule of thumb is that, the more advanced the age at reproductive maturity, the more highly evolved the being.* Age at puberty coincides with age at full reproductive maturity for some species, but not all.

For instance, the beast human reaches puberty at approximately age 13. For a few years, his semen may be somewhat wanting in potency, but by age 17, he is as potent as he will ever be. Thus, we can conclusively say that he is reproductively mature at age 17.

The true human reaches puberty at about 12 years of age. She certainly may become pregnant any time after this age, but she is much less likely to become pregnant and more likely to miscarry between the ages of 12 and 23 than she is after the age of 23, given the same frequency of opportunity. Thus, a woman is not reproductively mature until the age of 23, a full eleven years beyond puberty, and a full six years later than the beast human. (Figure 3.4)

Restrictions on Breeding Potential

The portion of an animal's life that is devoted to breeding hints strongly at the animal's evolutionary status. More time spent in breeding equals less time available for higher pursuits. So, the more restrictions nature has imposed on an animal's breeding potential, the more evolvement credit it can be granted. The adult hairworm, for example, does nothing but breed—it doesn't even eat. Consequently, the hairworm's evolutionary status is nothing short of embarrassing.

---

* Fitemaster, Genevieve, *The Scientist's Compendium of Adages, Quips, Quotes, and Maxims.* (New York: Heritage Press, 1978).

EVOLUTIONARY FEATURE 10
Age at Reproductive Maturity

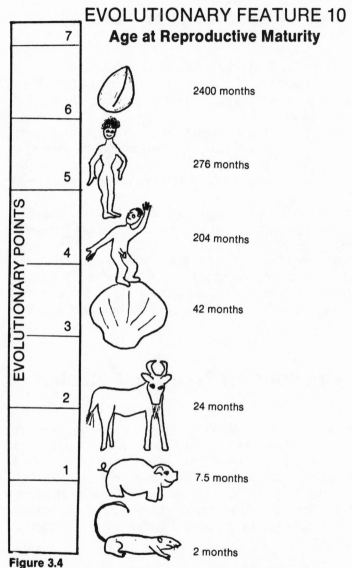

2400 months

276 months

204 months

42 months

24 months

7.5 months

2 months

Figure 3.4
The enviable restraint of the ocean bottom dwelling clam.
The average ocean bottom dwelling clam reaches reproductive maturity at 200 years of age—177 years later than the average true human. This marvelous mollusk is an obvious dark horse candidate for the distinguished evolutionary throne in a coming eon.
The shameful incontinence of the rat.
The rat reaches reproductive maturity at the ages of two months.
Compare this deplorable record with the other species above.

Reproductive Span/Life Span Ratio

Specialists other than myself have noted that the total period of life which is potentially procreative for any animal provides one important measurement of degree of evolvement.*

For instance, the average true human has a life span of about 70 years; she is reproductively capable about 30 of those years. This yields a Reproductive Span/Life Span (RS/LS) Ratio of 3/7 for the true human. That leaves the true human totally free of reproductive concerns to pursue higher interests for well over half of her life.

Compare this ratio with the beast human's. He also lives approximately 70 years, but is potentially procreative for about 60 of them. This yields a rather primitive RS/LS Ratio of 6/7. Although 6/7 is hardly a ratio to be proud of, it still gives him a healthy edge over the chinchilla and the mouse, as you can see in Figure 3.5.

Other Restrictions on Breeding Potential

The RS/LS Ratio provides a gross indication of a species' breeding potential, but finer measurements of breeding potential within the reproductive span are possible.

Non-human beasts. The majority of animals are blessed with breeding seasons which limit the time they devote to breeding activities to a mere fraction of their total reproductive life span. We monitored the breeding activities of several such beasts in our laboratories, ranging from our common tesselated racerunners with their modest two month breeding season to our dried fruit beetles who accomplished virtually nothing but breeding during their veritable twelve month orgy.

Beast humans. The breeding potential of the beast human is so great as to be incalculable. He is potentially reproductively capable almost every waking moment of his reproductive life span. He has no breeding season; his coitus is always fertile. Some small credit may be extended the beast human for the refractory phase

* Marthwhit-Chippenhammer, Laurie Ann, "What Your Reproductive Potential Says About Your Social Status," *Young American Parent*, July, 1976.

EVOLUTIONARY FEATURE 11
Reproductive Span/Life Span Ratios

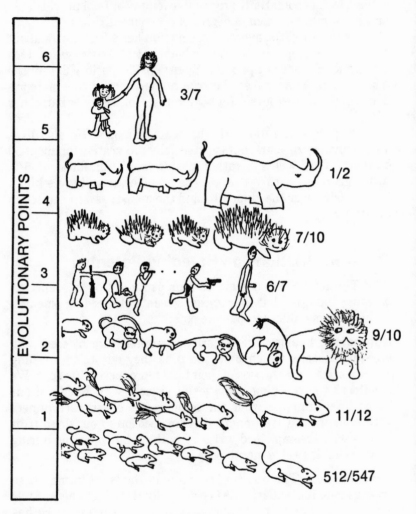

Figure 3.5

following ejaculation. At such times, Lloyd is barely capable of breathing, much less breeding.

True humans. Although she has no breeding season, the true human has been highly favored by nature with a number of other restrictions on breeding potential. A resounding 95% of her coital episodes are infertile since they occur between ovulations, during pregnancy, before puberty, or after menopause. She is blessed with infrequent ovulation, a long gestation period, adolescent suppressed fertility, relative post-partum sterility, and a relation between nutrition and reproduction which makes the inadequately nourished true human less susceptible to pregnancy than the well nourished one. Food evidently nourishes the higher primary functions in the true human before her secondary, reproductive ones.*

As you can see in Figure 3.6, the evolutionary disparity between true humans and beast humans on this feature could hardly be greater.

Fetal Wastage

It is generally believed that fetal wastage—miscarriage of conceptus—is higher among the lower animals than the higher ones.

Non-human beasts. Trimmer's abortion study** was too casual an undertaking to provide reliable fetal wastage data for the species she observed. The only solid numbers we have come from amateur zoologist Antonia Castillo de Parma, and even her study is derived from a very narrow sample of beasts (skunks, llamas, pigs, sheep, armadillos, and goats) that lived on her brother's farm.

---

* Meyeravend, Jocelyn, "Anatomic Destiny of Nutrients in a Minimally Adequate Diet," *Nutritional Digest,* vol. 4, no. 3, 1975.

** Trimmer, Valerie Agnes, "Some Observations on Spontaneous Abortion in Squirrels, Mice, Bats, Toads, and Shetland Ponies," *Right to Life Newsletter,* July, 1976.

EVOLUTIONARY FEATURE 12
Breeding Restrictions Within Reproductive Span

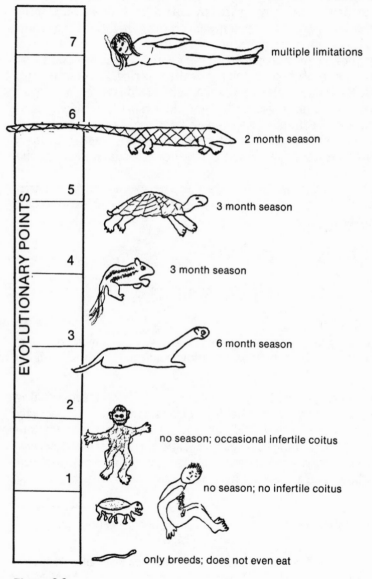

7 — multiple limitations

6 — 2 month season

5 — 3 month season

4 — 3 month season

3 — 6 month season

2 — no season; occasional infertile coitus

1 — no season; no infertile coitus

only breeds; does not even eat

EVOLUTIONARY POINTS

Figure 3.6

EVOLUTIONARY FEATURE 13
Fetal Wastage Rates

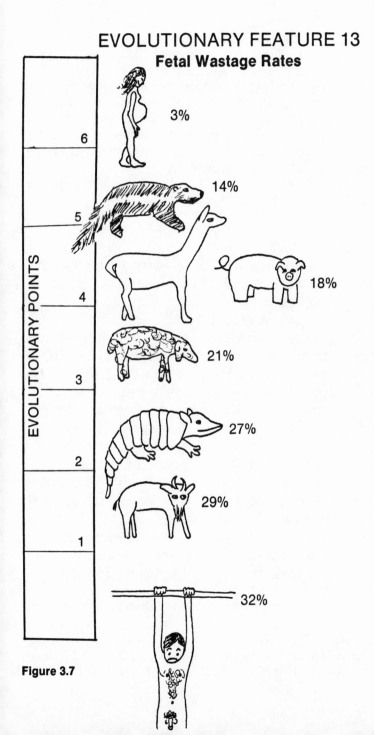

Figure 3.7

On the other hand, research on both the beast human and true human species is readily available. At least 125 and possibly 150 beast human males are conceived for every 100 true human females. But up to one third of the males conceived are so defective or excessively frail that they do not survive beyond the fetal stages. Consequently, even though 25-50% more males are conceived than females, only 6% more males are born than females. Soon after birth, the females begin to outnumber the males, and they increase their majority at every stage in life thereafter.*

The beast human scores so low on this evolutionary feature that he is in danger of falling off of Figure 3.7.

Summary

All of the species who have earned evolutionary points in our first three chapters are arranged in evolutionary order in the summary Figure 3.8.

As you can see from this table, there is more than a 3 point EPA discrepancy between the true human and the beast human. Lest any lay person think that this is an insignificant gap, I hasten to point out that in no other species where the two sexes have been rated separately for EPA has there ever been greater than a .63 difference, and the normal discrepancy is between .17 and .32.** If one sex of a species is more highly evolved than its partner in number of gametes produced, for example, the other sex is more highly evolved in age at reproductive maturity or degree of cerebral dominance or some other characteristic. It is therefore quite obvious that the human female population—largely true human—must be a separate species from the human male—largely beast human—population.

---

* Plassmeier, Diane, "Does Hardiness Indicate Highness?" *Magazine of Scientific Mysteries,* October, 1973.

** Sims, Margot H. and Diane Plassmeier, "Similarity of Intersexual EPA's Within Sample Species as Evidence of the Reliability of the EPA Scoring System," *Measurement: A Magazine for Measurers,* August, 1973.

Evolutionary Point Averages [EPAs] of Rated Species

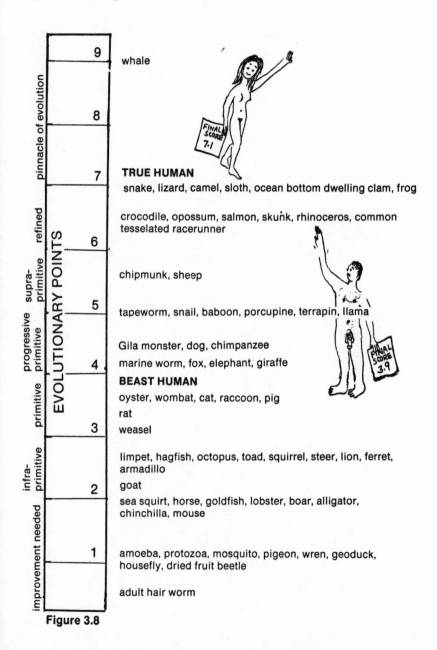

whale

TRUE HUMAN
snake, lizard, camel, sloth, ocean bottom dwelling clam, frog

crocodile, opossum, salmon, skunk, rhinoceros, common tesselated racerunner

chipmunk, sheep

tapeworm, snail, baboon, porcupine, terrapin, llama

Gila monster, dog, chimpanzee
marine worm, fox, elephant, giraffe
BEAST HUMAN
oyster, wombat, cat, raccoon, pig
rat
weasel

limpet, hagfish, octopus, toad, squirrel, steer, lion, ferret, armadillo
goat
sea squirt, horse, goldfish, lobster, boar, alligator, chinchilla, mouse

amoeba, protozoa, mosquito, pigeon, wren, geoduck, housefly, dried fruit beetle

adult hair worm

Figure 3.8

chapter 4

The Sexuo-
Psychological
Evidence

There is no end to the variety of what people find sexually stimulating. Jeannette and Mark LeFevre, my former next door neighbors, like to copulate in laundromat clothes dryers; my Aunt Veranda becomes impassioned when she rolls out pie crust (though she swore she would deny it if I had the audacity to make it public); my gay cousin Victor has only one orgasm a year—on Good Friday when he nails a volunteer Christ figure to a cross in the wilds of New Mexico. But all sexual preferences—common or uncommon—fall into two broad categories: physical and emotional.

"Emotion" is a recent evolutionary development. It does not appear on the evolutionary ladder until the mammalian rungs. When someone is called "cold-blooded" or "a cold fish," the implication is clear. That person's emotional capacity is comparable to a fish's or alligator's, animals not capable of even simple emotional states.

The ill-evolved beast human, naturally, has very limited emotional capacity. Consequently, sexual stimulation and satisfaction for him must come largely from the physical sector. His sexual behavior and habits confirm this.

The Fetishism Tendency: F.T.

When some lower animals—particularly ducks and geese—are born, they fixate on the first moving object they see and forever after relate to that object as "mother." This is called *imprinting*. A very similar phenomenon called *fetishism* (technically, the *fetishism tendency* or *F.T.)* occurs among beast humans, but not normally at birth and only rarely with their mothers. Here is an example of how it works.

Jerry N. experienced his first ejaculatory episode in his mother's closet, where she happened to have stored her red leather purse. He has never been able to reach climax again except in the presence of a red leather purse.

Jerry's case is typical. In some manner too primitive to be well understood, a sex-neutral stimulus *imprints* itself on the sex center of the beast human brain during the pivotal (often the initial) sexual episode. In the same way that a basketball can forever play the role of "mommy" for a duckling, red leather purses can become the *sine qua non* of sexual excitement for the beast human. (Figure 4.1)

Figure 4.1 It has been suggested that the greater incidence of fetishism among men than women indicates a throwback to avian origins in the former. (Catts, Gabrea, "The Birds and the Bees and Your Husband," *Bluebook,* September 1975; Tidbitt, Willie Jo, "Darwinism and Fetishism," *Sexual Inquiry,* vol. 42, no. 5, 1973.)

We interviewed 388 heterosexual and 73 homosexual male beast humans on this subject. At least 303 of the respondents had fetishes. Morris K. was typical.

> I don't know how some of those fine-looking dollies can walk around in low-heeled shoes. It makes them look about as attractive as collies. Hell, I'd rather fuck high heels without a woman than a woman without high heels.

Philip L. described his sexual relationship with his wife in glowing terms.

> Rhonda always takes a big pipe wrench to bed with her at night,
> and on special occasions, like my birthday and our anniversary,
> she lies naked with it under our bathroom sink.

Gay respondent Bernard F., a Young Republican, is only aroused by men who wear leftist political buttons.

> "Power to the People" has always been my favorite, but "Free
> Huey" or "Stop the Draft" or even "Save the Whales" will do
> the trick.

All of these men have fetishes, but none of them recognizes them as such. For instance, when we asked Jerry if he would call his fondness for red leather purses a fetish, he just laughed good-naturedly. "No, I'm not abnormal. Red leather purses are just sexy." (It is worth noting that Jerry can finely discriminate between real leather and plastic imitations. He finds the plastic imitations repulsive.)

Most respondents were not so genial when we asked if they thought they had fetishes. High-heels-loving Morris's answer was typical. "Are you calling me a pervert?" His belligerent gestures prevented our pursuing the subject any further. (Figure 4.2)

Though these men present somewhat extreme cases, all beast humans are afflicted* with some degree of the Fetishism Tendency (F.T.). Male homosexual fetishes appear to be more diverse and

Figure 4.2   Men can develop fetishes for almost anything.

---

* Perhaps "afflicted" is a poor word choice here, since fetishism is natural in most males. We don't stigmatize ducklings by saying they are "afflicted" with imprinting. However, a more suitable term does not present itself.

unpredictable than heterosexual ones, so we performed our fetish research on the heterosexual group.

We discovered that these men could be predictably stimulated by any randomly selected members of the female sex displaying particular superficial signals. For one man it may be blondeness, for another earrings, for another long legs. "Superficial" is the key word here. The beast human does not develop fetishes or even mild sexual preferences for qualities like intelligence or generosity, nor will the absence of these more profound qualities interfere with the sexual appeal of a woman.

In fact, the woman is quite incidental in evoking sexual interest in beast humans; the physical signals alone are sufficient.

After doing some shopping in town one day, I propped a new mop up next to me in my sportscar and headed back to the Center. As I picked up speed, the wind caught the tresses of the blonde mop. Wolf whistles and cat-calls followed "us" all the way back to Bleeding Heart.

Obviously, the mop's admirers were not responding to any of her higher human qualities. They were merely displaying the very common long blonde hair fetish. (Figure 4.3)

Figure 4.3   Even this ordinary household mop can inspire sexual frenzy in beast humans.

The Victorian practice of dressing furniture legs in little bloomers or pantaloons may seem ludicrous to some of us. But perhaps our Victorian foremothers were simply more sensitive to fetishes than we, and spared many leg-fetished men the unspeakable embarrassment of telltale trouser bulges at tea parties by hiding those stimulating gams from view. (Figure 4.4)

Figure 4.4   Many of us would not find this nude table very erotic.

In striking contrast to the fetish-prone beast human, the true human is sexually stimulated by a complex emotional state called "love," and is therefore fetish-immune.

The Promiscuity Urge: P.U.

Monogamy is unnatural and unattractive to the beast human, due in part, perhaps, to his fetishism. After all, a particular batch of red hair or a particular round buttocks becomes dull rather quickly. The boredom leads him to look for another partner, with more curls, or maybe a slimmer waist. He shares this trait with the male moth, which is attracted only by virginity; once he has deflowered a lady moth, he completely loses interest in her and pursues another virgin. (Figure 4.5)

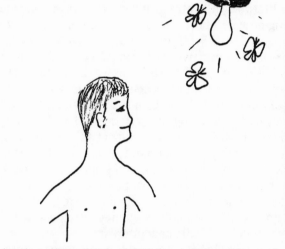

Figure 4.5 It has been hypothesized that the male beast human's passion for virginity reflects a hereditary link with the moths. Oldmann, Marie Gate, "Making Evolutionary Sense of the Virginity Quest in Man and Moth," *Evolution Today,* vol. 15, no. 9, 1977.)

The need for variety of sexual partners creates a real hardship for the male beast human since courtship is time-consuming, prostitutes are expensive, and rape is a crime. The movement away from farm life and into the cities during this century has compounded his sexual frustration. The sheep and goats which provided the rural male with so much variety in his sexual diet are not easily available in our urban centers.

Conversely, the naturally monogamous true human female, stimulated by more obscure (particularly in males) and complex non-physical qualities like trust, tenderness, and intellect, is not quickly bored with her mate—though she is often discouraged. She is stimulated by the belief that these qualities exist in her partner. This false belief contributes to the ironic, irreconcilable difference the two species exhibit in the area of the Promiscuity Urge (P.U.).

For the most part, only the homosexuals are happy. Gay men

prowl about, snatching one another out of bars and toilets and parks for innumerable titillating half-hour relationships. Lesbians establish intimate, stable love affairs which last years, decades, or a lifetime. In contrast, heterosexuals are engaged in a perpetual tug-of-war. They go steady, break up, live together, move out, get engaged, call it off, get married, have affairs, get divorced in an endlessly repetitive, pathological cycle. (Figure 4.6)

Heterosexual disturbances are rampant. Droves of men and women flock to sex therapists and write to lovelorn columnists for solutions to their problems. Professionals have been somewhat misguided, however, in advising that truly satisfying sex can only be accomplished with one mate at a time and on a long-term basis— a feat of which at least half the partners are incapable. No wonder hetero-sex is such a mess. Since he has a constitutional inability to comprehend, appreciate, or be stimulated by the more complex and deep qualities of the true human female, the beast human desires and must continually seek new partners with new superficial attributes to kindle new interest.

The male beast human is quite like most other animals in his quest for variety, and also like very young children, who tire of playthings long before they have begun to comprehend their complexity. For example, my studies indicate that a rat will become bored with a piano much more quickly than a chimpanzee (even if the piano is scaled to rat size). The rat will run across the keys once or twice and be done with it, while the chimpanzee will ordinarily "play" the instrument some. (Figure 4.7)

So great is his desire for variety in sexual partners, and so easily is he stimulated, that the beast human will commonly engage in sexuo-reproductive activity with complete strangers, sometimes outright victims, often paid receptacles, and occasionally volunteers. This is a shocking fact, considering that most of the other primates and sub-primates will have sexuo-reproductive relations only with familiar animals. This is true even in species such as rabbits and deer in which mateships (long-term, monogamous associations) do not exist. There are a few species, such as the common house mouse and the Norway rat (note the repeated rodent link) who—like the male beast human—seek and have intercourse with total strangers.

The Promiscuity Urge (P.U.) is a clear manifestation of physicality as opposed to emotion in sexual temperament. Emo-

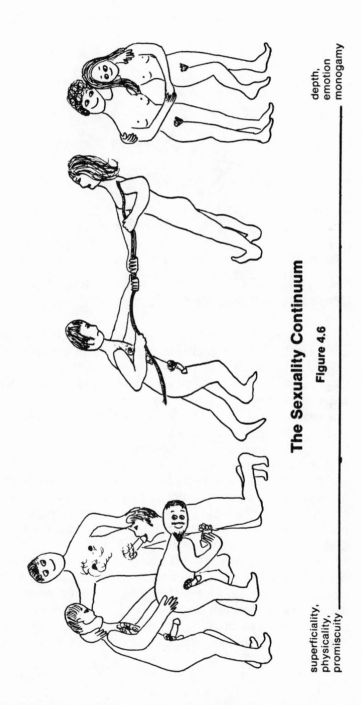

The Sexuality Continuum

Figure 4.6

superficiality,
physicality,
promiscuity

depth,
emotion
monogamy

Figure 4.7   The chimpanzee demonstrates greater innate skill at the piano than does the rat. (Sims, Margot H., "Promiscuity and Piano Playing: An Unexpected Correlation," *Journal of Sexual Anomalies,* vol. 1, no. 1, 1977.)

tional ties are possible only with close loved ones, but physical ties are possible with any available creature. If an animal chooses to engage in sexuo-reproductive acts with unfamiliar animals, it is clear that emotional stimulation is unimportant. The more unfamiliar the chosen partner (for instance, a total stranger as opposed to a casual acquaintance), the less emotional attachment is present and the less highly evolved is the animal.

The number of sexual partners and the frequency of change in partners determine the P.U. in animals, ranging from species which change partners with every episode of intercourse and have intercourse with total strangers, to species which are monogamous, often having but a single sex partner in a lifetime. The beast human and true human appear at the lowest and highest extremes of this Index, as you can see in Figure 4.8.

Since the identity of the sexual partner is unimportant to the beast human, one sexual encounter is usually indistinguishable from another for him. Memorable encounters are those in which he uses a greater than usual amount of force, inflicts a greater than usual degree of humiliation, or has a better than average looking partner. In addition, he will usually remember his first encounter and his most recent one.

Promiscuity Index

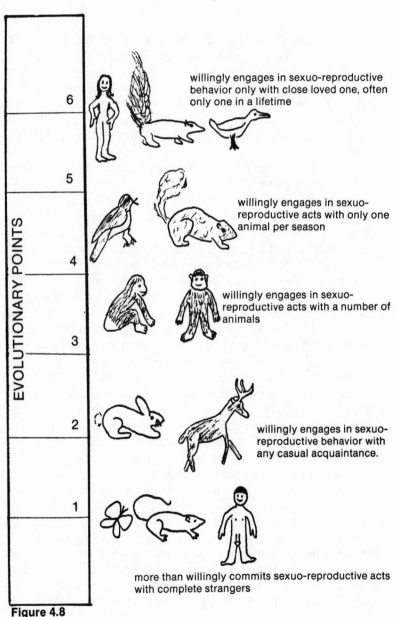

6 — willingly engages in sexuo-reproductive behavior only with close loved one, often only one in a lifetime

5 / 4 — willingly engages in sexuo-reproductive acts with only one animal per season

4 / 3 — willingly engages in sexuo-reproductive acts with a number of animals

2 — willingly engages in sexuo-reproductive behavior with any casual acquaintance.

1 — more than willingly commits sexuo-reproductive acts with complete strangers

EVOLUTIONARY POINTS

Figure 4.8

The Masturbation Impulse: M.I.

It is a documented fact, as well as common knowledge, that males (beast humans) are more prone to the Masturbation Impulse (M.I.) than are females (true humans). (Note the presence of "Have you committed a sin with yourself?" on the confessional prompting cards of Catholic boys and its absence on the cards of Catholic girls.) What is that quality of masturbation that makes it more appealing and satisfying to the beast human than to the true human?

Since there is no partner in masturbation, there can be no emotional interchange; there is only the manipulation of one's own body parts. Remembering what we have learned about the importance of superficiality and the insignificance of partner identity in the sexual arousal of beast humans, it is easy to see that a manipulative technique, possibly accompanied by fantasy, would be more satisfying to them than it would be to true humans, who would tend to favor a genuine emotional exchange.

The seemingly unquenchable desire to manipulate one's genitals is so strong among male beast humans that threats of eternal damnation, imbecility, insanity, and sundry physical ills resulting from it have done little over the years to snuff out its practice.

Some of our heterosexual masturbation subjects actually preferred onanism to partner sex. Ernest G. stated that he didn't "like being dependent on other people—especially chicks. This way I don't need anybody but Ernie!" Chuck V. says he has to "budget my time and money very carefully. Women take too much of both." Larry N. had the most common rationale: "Arousing Vicky is so much trouble, and she insists on it. It takes all the fun out of that kind of sex, so I like beating off a lot better."

It is difficult to draw conclusions about masturbatory intentions in non-human animals. Since many of them lack the necessary dexterity to masturbate, it would be unfair to rank species according to onanistic frequency. After all, should I give my little oyster Marina credit for not masturbating when she might very much desire to do so had she the means? And how can I tell whether my six goats are merely attending itches, or whether they have true masturbatory intent when they rub their genitalia against a stone or a tree? There does seem to be a real deliberateness in the manner in which my dog Muffin licks his reproductive organs. Most men are not limber enough to behave similarly, but are we to assume they would not like to? (Figure 4.9)

Figure 4.9 Some animals are better equipped for self-stimulation than others.

Among creatures able to masturbate, orally or manually, the more lowly evolved species masturbate more frequently then the more highly evolved species. And true humans, who certainly have the wherewithal to do a splendid job of it, masturbate only occasionally, presumably because of the lack of an emotional component in the practice.

Some male yogis are limber enough to have oral sex with themselves. There is reason to suspect that orgasm thus induced might be a favorite shortcut to Nirvana. (Norris, Robyn, *Philosophical Expurgations,* Belfry Press, Cambridge, 1981.)

The Force Factor: F.F.

Force is a primal impulse whose origins and reason for development are obscure. Some authorities have conjectured that, eons ago, in order to prevent the even then less beastly female from shirking relations which were for her merely reproductive (as well as abhorrent) rather than sexual in nature, innate brutish force was Darwinially developed in the male to insure frequent reproductive contact.

Since practically no females had an interest in serving as sperm receptacles, force became so closely associated with sexual relations that it became desirable in and of itself. By the time it had lost its biological necessity, its psychological necessity had become entrenched.

The Force Factor (F.F.) is present in beast humans only—never in true humans. Ordinarily, an individual whose sexual temperament is F.F.-dominated likes to use force to wrest sex from someone else, but, paradoxically, satisfaction in having sex forcibly wrested from oneself is F.F.-dominated as well.

The F.F. comprises a good deal of the male arousal and release mechanism, and yet many of the more respected sexologists and sex therapists remain naively blind to its existence, probably because they are predominantly true humans themselves. Since the F.F. plays no part in the sexual functioning of most women, they continue to overlook its importance to men. Also, there is a continued reluctance on the part of these professionals to learn from pornographers, pimps, and prostitutes, who are all far better versed in the quirks of male sexuality than they are.

The Degradation Compulsion: D.C.

The desire to degrade one's sex partner is a refined extension of the Force Factor. This sexual preference is totally unique to the beast human species, most likely because other species endowed with the Force Factor, such as mice, have limited language ability and are probably not able to comprehend the abstract quality of the Degradation Compulsion (D.C.).

With their thorough knowledge of the D.C.-oriented beast human sexual nature, pornographers put Kinsey, Masters and Johnson, Reuben, and all the other Establishment sex gurus to shame. Porn publishers' appreciation for the sexual importance of degradation is so complete that they routinely provide their aspiring writers with step-by-step formulae for creating sure-fire, bestselling "deggie" novels. For instance, here is an excerpt from a deg-formula issued by Greenleaf's Keyhole Classics.

> Early in the book, reveal the antagonists' intentions of debasing the heroine, their desire to bring her down to their level of gross salacity.

Here lies the key to understanding the beast human's consuming need to degrade the true human. He senses and resents her superiority; by humiliating her, he punishes her for her evolutionary advantage and makes her his lowly equal.   .

We read abbreviated deggie stories to incoming pools of subjects at the Center to separate the true humans from the beast humans. As a screening device, this technique has proved almost 100% reliable. By the pivotal third paragraph in each story, species identification is clear. Beast human males have full-blown bulges in their trousers, and beast human females have activated the lubrication-sensitive electrodes implanted in their chairs.

Our deg-stories are standard fare. One concerns a fifteen-year-old virgin beauty taken from boarding school by her father for a weekend visit to his secluded farm. By the end of the second paragraph, he has raped his daughter in his carriage; by the end of the third paragraph, the mentally deranged stable boy has tied her up and had anal sex with her; by the close of the fourth paragraph, a field hand has discovered her enticing a sheep to lick her genitals and punishes her by binding her to a tractor and forcing her to suck on his penis while he penetrates her with a cucumber. The sixth and final paragraph finds our heroine begging her father to fill her only available orifice while the moronic stable boy and sadistic field hand keep her vagina and mouth busy.

In another of our deggie favorites, an aristocratic Hindu

woman, who believes cattle are sacred, is made to "eat beef"—commit fellatio with a steer—in the important third paragraph. She has an orgasm in spite of herself. Of course, these descriptions are only the highlights, but they illustrate the type of humiliation which is so sexually titillating to the beast human species.

The Orgasm Correlation: O.C.

Commonly, "orgasm" and "sexual satisfaction" are used almost interchangeably. There is not very much wrong with this usage when talking about beast humans, but it is inaccurate when applied to true humans as well.

Beast human orgasm/sexual satisfaction is simply and directly correlated with adequate physical stimulation. True human orgasm/sexual satisfaction is correlated with adequate emotional stimulation. But the correlation is not a simple one. Women may experience orgasm without satisfaction, satisfaction without orgasm, dissatisfaction without orgasm, and satisfaction with orgasm. We know that emotional stimulation plays a part in determining the outcome of true human sexual encounters, but we do not know how it works or what other variables may also be at play. Our study subjects attest that sexual satisfaction with orgasm is even sweeter than sexual satisfaction without orgasm, so there appears to be some tenuous connection between the two in true humans.

The Post-Orgasmic Phase: P.O.P.

Because the correlation between orgasm and satisfaction (O.C.) is not the strict one among true humans that it is among beast humans, one would expect the Post-Orgasmic Phase (P.O.P.) to be markedly different in the two. And it is.

A post-orgasmic and/or post-satisfaction true human female

frequently desires and is certainly capable of experiencing additional orgasm and/or satisfaction immediately following an episode of same, provided that sufficient emotional stimulation is still present, which for heterosexuals it usually isn't, because the vehicle for emotional stimulation is ordinarily snoring like a hibernating bear by her side soon after his final orgasmic grunts are uttered. (Figure 4.10)

Unfortunately for aroused women, the beast human neither desires nor is capable of further sexual activity once he has completed his single ejaculatory spasm. He enters a dormant phase which varies in length from twenty minutes to nine days, and during dormancy, his reactions to sexual stimuli range from indifference to revulsion.

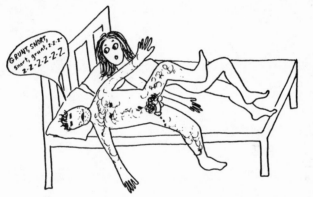

Figure 4.10   When recordings of the ejaculatory grunts of baboons were interspersed with those of male beast humans, 92.3% of sexually experienced heterosexual human females could not distinguish between the two. (Plassmeier, Diane, "The Significance of Primate Grunts," *Averbal Communication Journal*, vol. 3, no. 4, 1976.)

Summary

Man's Sexuality is characterized by the F.T., the P.U., the M.I., the F.F., and the D.C. His O.C. is simple and his P.O.P. is as predictable as a bear's. Woman's sexuality cannot be described with acronyms.

chapter 5

The Case from
Sexuo-Sociology

Given the very disparate sexual natures of beast humans and true humans, the social institutions and ideals they have evolved cannot possibly accommodate them both satisfactorily.

Courtship

Members of the same species are innately interested in identifying and cooperating with other members of their species for the purpose of mating, and complementary courtship behavior enables them to do so. Since beast humans and true humans are not very closely related species, it is no surprise that they employ courtship behaviors which are anti-complementary. (Figure 5.1)

Figure 5.1   Elaborate courtship behaviors enable animals to identify members of their own species for purposes of mating.

This is an obvious clue that human beings could not possibly all be one species. Even without all of the other evidence, this fact should long ago have given scientists pause. There are two species here, and they are relaying confusing and offensive signals to each other in their bungling efforts to select mates.

The male beast human makes crude, explicit overtures, suggesting fleeting coital liaisons. He likes to make initial contact by screaming obscenities from speeding cars or by accosting women on street corners or in other public places. The female true human feels revulsion at these overtures. She prefers discreet introductions through trusted acquaintances or gradual, non-committal exposure in a classroom, workplace, or other sex-neutral environment. One favors the quick and overt; the other the slow and subtle. If our study of biology and evolution has any application at all for humankind, this anti-complementarity should be perilous to the perpetuation of the two species. (Figure 5.2)

Figure 5.2 Beast human courtship behavior is often distasteful to true humans.

Similarly, once initial contact has been accomplished, one species/sex favors immediate sexuo-reproductive activity, while the other favors a delayed, sexually fulfilling journey toward emotional commitment. Compromises and negotiations on this factor alone have caused incalculable misery and innumerable pair breakups. Very few pairs would ever survive this period of attachment were it not for the Force Factor (F.F.) contribution from the beast human and the desperate loneliness contribution from the true human. Without these, the two species would have become seriously depopulated by this era, if not already extinct.

The minutiae of courtship are no less contradictory. One

species would prefer to give gifts of liquor, but gives flowers instead because he has been taught (he does not know innately, as he would if he were a member of the same species) that the other sex prefers flowers and is thus made more willing to compromise on other points (which he considers more important anyway) because of this trifling concession on his part. One species would prefer to celebrate a special occasion at a wrestling match while the other would favor an intimate fireside tête-à-tête.

True humans cope with this anti-complementarity in several ways. The lucky ones are lesbians, unconcerned with the inadequacies of male courtship. Some become spinsters and nuns. The unfortunate heterosexual majority must convince themselves that the decoy behavior which the male learns (like giving flowers, making promises, holding hands) reflects his true feelings. This ability to fool herself about the true nature of her suitor is greatly facilitated by the female true human's capacity for fantasy.

The Fantasy of the Evolved Male. When our lives are very difficult or deficient, we tend to make believe that things are better. It is this ability to fantasize that brings comfort to a lonely child, orgasm to a frustrated adolescent, and relief to a stranded mountain climber. This escape from reality can develop into mental illness, but more often serves to prevent serious mental disturbance.

Without the ability to fantasize, women would certainly be more insane than they ordinarily are. With their fantasy of "Let's pretend men are true human beings," many can go for long periods of time with remarkable mental stability. Soap operas, novels, movies, women's magazines—all of them portray very highly evolved, lovestruck men as typical of the sex and bolster the "Let's pretend" efforts.

The fantastic male is always in love with and devoted to one woman, whom he is pursuing with fervent ardor. He is religious and loves babies. He is offended by girlie magazines. He is hardworking, vigorous, and ethical. He is very handsome to boot. He is frank and friendly; there is nothing secretive in his manner, though a touch of mystery is sometimes present. He never smirks and his mouth doesn't water.

It is not difficult to write the magazine stories and the Gothic novels incorporating the fantasies, because there does not have to be a flesh and blood portrayal of the evolved male. The portrayal of the evolved male is easy in soap operas, where unconvincing acting is not a detraction at all, but a convention easily accommodated in the viewing fantasizer's mind.

Movies, however, present somewhat more of a problem, because even the best actors find it extremely taxing to simulate true human feelings. Generally, gay men do a much better job of impersonation than straight men, so they are often chosen for the more romantic, overtly heterosexual roles. Cruelly, cheap newspapers or even a woman's own friend may hint that her favorite love idol is gay. This can seriously interfere with a well-established fantasy pattern. (Figure 5.3)

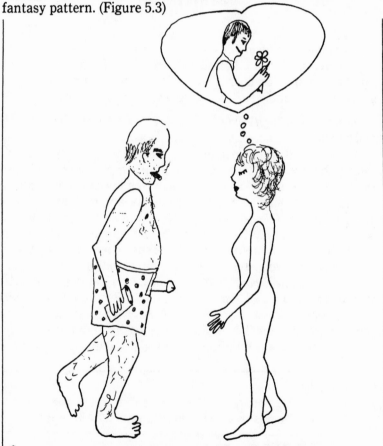

Figure 5.3 Fantasies enable many true human females to cope more satisfactorily with their lives.

This proclivity for fantasy is in fact a survival mechanism created by women to compensate for the shortcomings of male beast humans. Without it, these shortcomings would so seriously interfere with courtship behavior that relatively few male-female alliances would ever take place. Still, courtship is a facet of true human-beast human relations to which species adaptation has been very poor.

Marriage

Marriage is one of the oldest, and probably the most universally revered, of the alliances between true humans and beast humans. Many marriage partners are only mildly miserable, but some are profoundly so. There are several reasons for this.

Selecting a Marriage Partner. In spite of his naturally promiscuous and shallow character, the average beast human likes to select permanent and semi-permanent mates. He ordinarily does not intend these mates to be exclusive, but simply more significant than his others. He also prefers a semi-permanent mate as insurance, so someone will always be at hand to minister to his sexual and domestic needs. It is also natural for the true human to seek a long-term mate, so the characteristic *per se* is shared by the two species. What are not shared are the criteria by which each judges prospective mates, as the following studies demonstrate.

In *The Evans Report**, the following description was submitted to 803 males and 792 females on a large Pacific Northwestern college campus. Each respondent was asked whether the following sentence struck him/her negatively or positively in describing a future mate: "Deaf and dumb and over-sexed and owns a liquor store."

Results:
male: 53% positive;   32% indifferent;   15% negative
female: 7% positive; 0.6% indifferent; 92.4% negative

* Evans, Jane and Jacqueline, "The Evans Report," in *Choosing a Mate.* (Seattle, WA: Kazian "How to Do It" series, vol. 16, 1976).

Conclusion: A majority of males and females differ in fundamental ways in regard to what they find desirable in a mate.

In *The Pirase Study**, 612 male and 680 female unmarried high school seniors were asked to rank seven traits from most desirable to least desirable in a mate.

Results:

male	female
1. good looks	1. tenderness
2. youth	2. companionship
3. sex expertise	3. education
4. humor	4. humor
5. education	5. sex expertise
6. companionship	6. youth
7. tenderness	7. good looks

Conclusion: Males and females have opposite priorities in features they desire in their mates. Even so, this gives them an equal interest in a sense of humor and not very disparate interests in sexual expertise and education.

The results of these studies inspired me to conduct an experiment of my own. My brother-in-law, Roscoe Treadwater, has operated a very successful computer dating service in the Bronx for nearly twenty years. Every month, Roscoe brings thousands of romance-hungry men and women together, using his patented Compatibility Index computer program. Nonetheless, he has never achieved an average Compatibility Index (C.I.) higher than 64.

I guaranteed Roscoe that, by making only one tiny change in his computer program, I could achieve an average C.I. of at least 90 on his next group of clients. He scoffed, but agreed to let me try. You can imagine Roscoe's surprise when, on my first attempt, I produced an average C.I. of 96. All I had done was eliminate information on gender from the computer's memory, so it had matched people solely on the basis of compatibility, without regard to their sex. As a result, men were paired with men and women with women, all very compatibly.

---

* Pirase, Petra, "The Pirase Study," in *Choosing a Mate. ibid.*

When he saw what I had done, Roscoe accused me of cheating. From a business point of view, I suppose he was right, for his clients would certainly have demanded their money back if he had matched them with members of their own sex.

These results dramatize the tragedy of true human hetero-sexuality. Most women want their lovers to be tender, companionable, passionate, *and* equipped with a penis. In fact, the penis appears to be the most important feature of all, since most women forego tenderness, companionship, and passion to get it.

No one understands why it is so important to the majority of women that their lovers have penises, nor why so many men are partial to lovers with vaginas. It is a puzzling area that warrants extensive research. Whatever its cause, this irrational addiction to opposite-sex genitalia presents a poignant obstacle to happy matings among 90% of the human population.

Although most harmonious human pairings are homosexual, a few healthy heterosexual matches result from the pairing of male beast humans with members of the tiny minority of female beast humans. There is astonishing balance in these relationships.

The desire to defile is perfectly matched with the desire to be degraded; the insistence that sex must be dirty is coupled with the

Figure 5.4   Beast human male traits and beast human female traits balance perfectly.

feeling that one's body is foul; the obsession to possess is balanced with a compulsion for security; the impulse to rape and beat is paired with marty.:dom and masochism; the inability to recognize superiority and refinement is met with a blessed absence of those qualities; lies and deceit are mated with dishonesty and guilt; boredom is balanced with quarrelsomeness and quarrelsomeness with boredom; the male's perception of the female in physical terms is matched with the female's consuming vanity. (Figure 5.4)

At the Center, I interviewed 41 satisfactorily married beast human females and learned that all each of them had really sought in a prospective husband was (1) a large penis, (2) a small mind, and (3) full pockets. These qualities are much more readily available than such true human traits as tenderness and emotional depth. Though the first and third items are not common, by any means, their reasonable facsimiles are fairly easy to find. Little wonder that beast human females are so much more successful at marriage than true human females. (Figure 5.5)

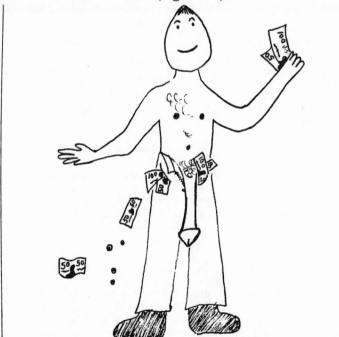

Figure 5.5   The ideal husband for a female beast human.

If any marriages are made in heaven, the beast human male-beast human female ones are. It is remarkable how these animals suit one another, exchanging their low "love" and meeting their mutual beast needs with pleasure and satisfaction. Their minds and hearts mesh as surely as their bodies. (It is an ironic quirk of nature, though perhaps fortunate in terms of survival, that the bodies, and nothing else, of beast humans mesh with true humans.) It is clear that there was design in matching the penis with the vagina; it was no accident. When one sees two lives as compatible as a penis and a vagina, one cannot help being struck with the correctness of the pairing

But if those marriages are made in heaven, the others are made in hell. The facts are bizarre and depressing. Thousands of beast humans who feel entitled to five minutes of sex every second night are married to true humans who want quiet, intimate talks and lovemaking into the wee hours of the morning; millions of tender-hearted true human creatures impart their deepest and most intimate hopes and secrets to their mates, and get belches in response; hundreds of thousands of sensitive females burst with tears because they feel true human anguish and pain, and their mates slap them around for being such babies.

Gloria Tumwater works as our bookkeeper at the Center for the Study of Human Types in Bleeding Heart. Hers typifies a true human-beast human marriage. Gloria gave us permission to quote a section from her divorce court transcript.

Judge: Mrs. Tumwater, does your husband give you his paycheck every week?
Gloria: Yes, but—it's only because he doesn't know how to cash checks. He makes me cash it for him and give him all the money.
Judge: Mrs. Tumwater, the court is very busy. Just yes or no is all the answer I need. Tell me, Mrs. Tumwater, does your husband ever have affairs with other women?
Gloria: Well, no—I don't think so, but—
Judge: Yes?
Gloria: Well, he—I know he's had sex with our German shepherd on several occasions.
Judge: Mrs. Tumwater, it's natural for a man to love his dog. I asked you about other women.
Gloria: Well, I—I don't think Heidi's the only one. I've found other dog hair—from an Afghan, I think—on his clothes, and—
Judge: Please, Mrs. Tumwater. So, your husband does not have affairs with other women. Does he ever strike you, with his

hand or some object?
Gloria: No, but he bites me pretty often...on—on my bottom. It's
the only way he can get an erection.
Judge: So, the answer is no, your husband does not beat you. He
also never has affairs with other women. He also hands over his
paycheck to you every week. Mrs. Tumwater, just what *is* your
complaint?
Gloria: Well, like I said....
Judge: Divorce denied. (sound of gavel) Next case.

Gloria's case is not exceptional. Because of the two separate
human species, the majority of true humans seek tenderness,
friendship, intimacy, respect, emotional depth with reciprocation,
communication, companionship, trust—in short, true human love.
For the heterosexual majority of them, there are no suitable mates,
no beings capable of meeting those needs and desires. Therefore,
they kill themselves off in alarming numbers, are confined to
institutions for the mentally infirm in droves, flock to therapy
sessions, form wailing groups among themselves—none of which
attempted solutions can even begin to solve the problem.

Male beast humans, even if they try earnestly and long (and a
few do), cannot provide for these needs of true humans any more
than a bull can produce milk. Seventy-five percent (75%) of all
marriage contracts are initiated—subtly or openly—by women,
and 75% of all divorce suits are brought by women—always openly.
Women know what they want; they are simply unable to get it.

Prostitution

Surely older than marriage, and only slightly less revered as a
male-female alliance, is prostitution.

During our study of prostitution, we found such stigma
attached to the word "prostitute" that in determining the prevalence of prostitution in a large, Midwestern city, we had to drop the
word itself from our questionnaire. We re-phrased all of the
questions so that we could discover which women, for economic
benefit, had engaged in sex which they hadn't enjoyed. To our utter
astonishment, we found that 100% of the adult female population

was practicing or had practiced prostitution.

For instance, there was Marian, the PTA president who was frigid, but found marriage more to her liking than a nine-to-five job. And Carla, who traded her virginity to Tommy for a date to the prom. And there was Dinah, the second grade teacher who loved children but didn't know her alphabet. She kept her job by bedding down with the principal.

Another recent survey deserves our attention. Seven hundred and eighty-two (782) male beast humans in the Cambridge, Massachusetts vicinity responded to a statement written on a plain brown wrapper, indicating whether they (1) agreed, (2) disagreed, (3) had no opinion, or (4) did not understand the statement. Eighty-three percent (83%) of respondents agreed with the statement that: "The prevalence of female prostitution is a natural and acceptable state of affairs." Six percent (6%) had no opinion, and 11% did not understand the question.*

I would have to agree with the majority opinion. With the sexual natures of true humans and beast humans so contradictory, female prostitution is natural, inevitable, and ineliminable—no matter how unsavory.

Rape

Probably the most ancient, but not always openly revered, male-female institution is rape. Some persons may object and say that rape is not an institution, but merely a crime. I disagree. Its antiquity, its universality, and its frequent occurrence have all but legitimized rape in the eyes of society.

Given the Force Factor (F.F.) and the Degradation Compulsion (D.C.), liking to rape is as natural to a beast human as liking ice cream is to a child.

In a survey of beast humans in Berkeley, California, 79% of the respondents believed: "There is no such thing as a female rape victim since alleged victims either outright invited the rape or at least enjoyed it." Twenty-one percent (21%) believed there were

---

* Veeroff, Ted, *et al,* "Brown Bag Inquiry #3: Prostitution," *American Lunch-Time Surveys,* Scallop Polls, Princeville, 1976.

sometimes victims. No one had no opinion, and everyone understood the question.*

True humans have suffered grievously from the rape impulse, but very little can be done to restrain it. Laws and curfews curb the impulse to some degree, but men just like to do it so much that the urge is not susceptible to strict control. Will all the threats and law enforcement in the world destroy a child's love of ice cream? Certainly not, and there are some who will undergo great risks to get it. Of course, with no restraints at all, it is only natural that they will absolutely gorge themselves.

The same is true of the male beast human. Many will not risk the law, but given impunity—as in wartime—they will certainly gorge themselves. The American nurses raped by the Japanese in WWII, the German frauleins raped by the Americans, and almost every other nationality raped by every other nationality in one war or another give some indication of the strength of the rape impulse.

These soldiers are primarily, of course, our own brothers, fathers, sons, uncles, and other good men. Unwholesome men are excluded from the military, so there can be no question but that all of these rapes are committed by good boys. The domestic rape rate decreases dramatically when only the misfits are left on native soil.

True humans remain remarkably naive about the dangerousness of the beast human species. They persist in believing that the impulse to rape (and otherwise abuse) true human females occurs only in a small minority of psychopathic men, when in truth it is present in almost all of them.

Mothers have thought it appropriate for years to warn their daughters about the dangers of rattlesnakes, bears, and scorpions when they go to camp or on natural history hikes. Yet the wounds, deaths, and other physical abuses done true humans by all other species combined are miniscule in comparison with the bodily damage inflicted on them by their natural predator, the beast human. (Figure 5.6)

---

* Kelley, Ervin, *et al,* "Brown Bag Inquiry #2: Rape," *American Lunch-Time Surveys,* Scallop Polls, Princeville, 1976.

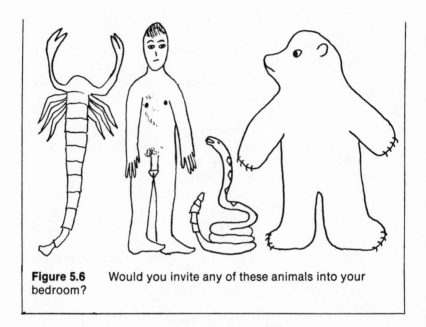

Figure 5.6   Would you invite any of these animals into your
bedroom?

Sexual Attitudes

Traditionally, women have not enjoyed sex, have felt shame in even speaking of it, and have in fact found it repulsive. Men have thought it dirty, beastly, and highly attractive. Recently, there has been a shift in the attitudes women are expected to have about sex.

Inexperienced, impressionable young women today are taught from a very young age that sex is the beautiful, natural, physical expression of a love which cannot be expressed or experienced in any other way; that sex is the vehicle for the most intimate communication between lovers; that sex will make their very souls sing. Their friends, their magazines and books, their sex education teachers, their elders—all have a role in forming this glowing notion of (hetero)sexuality. By the time an innocent young thing has reached the age when she is likely to fall in love for the first time, she has come to expect something almost ethereal in beauty from sexual union.

And she does fall in love. Soon after, trembling with anticipation, she approaches the love bed with her beloved. Suddenly, she feels rough, hairy hands mauling her clothing and body; she sees glazed eyes leering at her; she feels a drooling mouth slobbering on her; and she hears an animal grunting in her ear. All at once, her chest is crushed and she can hardly breathe, but it's over so fast that she is not endangered from lack of oxygen. Before she knows what has happened, her partner is snoring at her side, sweat dripping from his body, and some tardy fluids still oozing from his penis. The young girl has just been introduced to beast human sex, and she has not found it very beautiful.*

When she has had time to recover, this typical, disappointed young girl wonders what is wrong that she has found sex so unexpectedly revolting and disgusting. She risks the labels of "old-fashioned," "frigid," and "abnormal" from her peers if she confesses to a loathing of sex or betrays a shame in speaking of it. Therefore, she does not reveal her true feelings, but decides she is maladjusted and suffering from some neurotic repression of her sexuality. To cure herself, she consults sex manuals, attends therapy groups, practices positive thinking—all in an effort to remove her psychological blocks so that she can enjoy sex in its natural beauty and wholesomeness.

But, of course, all the positive thinking in the world cannot make beast human sex attractive to a true human. Beast human sex is degrading and ugly to a true human. True human sex can deliver the promised rewards of exquisite rapture and unparalleled intimacy, but true human heterosexual sex is nearly impossible to come by.

---

* In her prize-winning essay, *Werewolves and Wedding Nights,* psycho-analyst Mari Lubbock explores the psychological consequences of lover-inflicted sexual trauma. "The knowledge of male bestiality is inborn in women; it reverberates through the female subconscious even *in utero,*" she claims. "The initial (hetero) sexual experience often pops the cork on the subconscious perception, forcing the woman to recognize male bestiality on a more conscious level. Thus springs the werewolf myth. Werewolf stories and movies fascinate and horrify women because, subconsciously, they are seeing their own lovers, fathers, brothers, and sons embodied in these dichotomous monsters." Lubbock makes extensive reference to the primary literature, such as: "Finally Mom Told Me Her Secret Nightmare—MY DADDY WAS A WEREWOLF!" *Lurid Romance,* April 1981; and, "When I Was Sweet and Innocent and 15, I WENT STEADY WITH A WEREWOLF!" *Secret Confessions,* October 1981.

Each newly disillusioned young woman takes her place among the throngs misinforming the uninitiated innocents. She joins their ranks for two very understandable reasons. First, she wishes to be thought normal, and can only be thought so if she professes the accepted view. Second, she does not wish to impair her own daughters' and other young women's chances of achieving sexual happiness by saddling them with her own warped and discredited ideas. She is like an army officer who hopes his pretense of bravery will inspire genuine bravery in his troops. In this way, the modern myth of the beauty of (hetero)sex is perpetuated among women.

Our foremothers were no better off than we as far as the probability of achieving sexual satisfaction is concerned, but at least they had the advantage of correct information and expectations in sexual matters.

For example, in 1929, J.P. Mavis asked 883 American women if they had received adequate preparatory instruction regarding sex. Over half said they had. Answers included: "Mother told me what I should expect. Submitting to my father's demands had been her cross to bear;" and "Men are nothing but animals;" and "Oh yes, I knew that men were beasts." (The remarkable insight of the latter two women is striking. However, they were speaking figuratively rather than literally, and probably never appreciated the implications of their discovery.) Even those in the study who answered that they had not received adequate instruction had probably been somewhat prepared for the marital state by the ominous shroud of silence which smothered the subject. At the very least, they had not been misinformed, as is the modern young girl.

It is impossible to obtain accurate statistics about sexual preparation of young women today because there is such a reluctance on the part of the modern woman to disabuse herself of the notion that the fault lies with herself—and not with her preparation—that she finds sex so revolting. It is safe to state, however, that the great majority of women today do not receive adequate preparatory instruction in sexual matters, and this lamentable fact is the more ironic because our modern society prides itself on disbursing sex information *more* freely than its forbears, not less.

The plain truth is that women who find beast human sex disgusting are perfectly normal, healthy individuals, and it is time that society again allowed them to admit their feelings openly.

Reverting to the traditional attitude would at least spare young girls the unspeakable cruelty of their disillusionment in the sexual sphere. However, abandoning the "sex is beautiful" philosophy and reverting to the traditional "sex is ugly" philosophy will not remedy the unfortunate fact that very few heterosexual women will ever achieve sexual happiness under the dual species condition. A more fundamental change is called for, one which will actually make female sexual satisfaction routinely possible.

The Double Standard

Related to the confusion about sexual attitudes is the so-called "double standard."

It has been recognized for centuries that promiscuousness, exoticness, and liberality in sexual behavior would coarsen a young woman. In contrast, promiscuity and libertinism have been totally acceptable behavior for the male, who is by nature coarse, and therefore immune to the coarsening effects of these influences. Because the true human mixes socially with beast humans, and because she believes herself to be of the same species as they, she occasionally protests that the dual morality—the so-called "double standard"—is unfair.

If she were not in such a singular evolutionary circumstance, the true human would take no more notice of the difference in the expectations concerning her own sexual conduct and that of the beast human's than she does between her own and her pet dog's.

Are geese even the slightest bit disturbed that cats are not reproved for their promiscuous lechery, while they would ostracize another goose for similar behavior? Does the monogamous fox envy the polygamous sea lion? Ridiculous. Every species has its own set of sexual mores which in no way affect or are answerable to those of other species. There is one set for dogs, one for true humans, another for turtles, another for beast humans, and so on. If it is unfair to have different codes of sexual morality for different species, then our current standard is far more than double—it is at least a thousand fold. (Figure 5.7)

Figure 5.7   The monogamous goose pays no heed to feline sex mores.

Of course, the minority of the female population which is beast human has a justifiable gripe. It is completely unfair to impose true human morals on these less highly evolved beings, just as it is unfair to ask the tiny minority of male true humans to grovel in the morals of the beast humans. Still the so-called "double standard" is perfectly reasonable for the large majority of the population. Two species, two standards.

The Feminist Fallacy. Some feminists demand equality of opportunity for sexual pleasure in the same way that they demand equality of pay and equality of employment opportunity. Their feeling is that men have always enjoyed sex in a free, uninhibited way, and that simple justice demands the same for women. At first glance, this view has some appeal. But given the double species with their double standard, it is easy to see that the desire for this kind of "equality" is fundamentally misguided. A carefree "sex is fun" philosophy is no more workable than a "sex is beautiful" philosophy in inter-species relationships.

Rôle Modeling. As we grow up from infancy, we all model ourselves after others: parents, teachers, movie stars. By looking at the individuals people choose to emulate, we can tell a great deal about what qualities those people admire.

Interestingly, beast humans often choose to emulate lower animals. During my hundreds of interviews with beast humans at the Center for the Study of Human Types, I was struck again and again by the frequency with which they evoked beasts as models to live by.

For instance, Dale V. thinks it is unnatural and wrong to allow physically deformed babies to live because "wolves kill their crippled young." Larry M. believes that interracial marriage should be a criminal offense because "red birds don't mate with bluebirds." Monroe T. claims that men should have several wives because "sea lions have harems."

It is beside the point that there are other species whose habits are quite contrary to those mentioned above. The mere fact that beast humans choose beasts as role models has persuaded me that, deep within the beast human psyche, there exists an innate recognition of his kinship with lower animals, his werewolf essence. He has a natural desire to follow the mores of beings he considers his equals. True human mores are beyond his emulation.

Summary

Our entire social order is in constant turmoil as a result of the two species trying to exist as one. Courtship behavior that is pleasurable to one sex is disgusting to the other; marriages are miserable and desperate; prostitution is universal, rape is rampant, and both are ineliminable; conflict over morality is incessant; unrealistic sexual expectations cause epidemic mental depression; and half the population reveres the mores of wolves, bluebirds, and sea lions.

These creatures—true humans and beast humans— are not partners by design, as are partners in other species. They are partners by some accident of evolution or catastrophe of history, about which we will speculate in the next chapter.

chapter 6

Evolutionists Explain

The two human species appear to be unique in the animal kingdom in respect to their having predominantly only one sex in each species. In all other species in which there are clearly differentiated sexes, the males and females have progressed and regressed at similar—perhaps identical—rates up and down the evolutionary ladder. Whether claw in claw, gill in gill, wing in wing, or hand in hand, these creatures have retained a sameness, an essential similarity to their mates. (Figure 6.1)

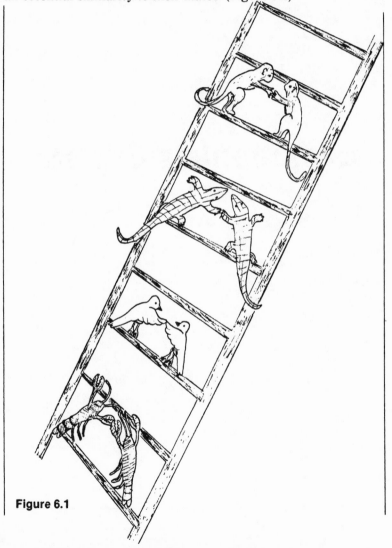

Figure 6.1

But something different happened among the humans, and the fact is, we simply don't know what that "something" was. It seems fairly clear that one of two broad evolutionary possibilities is at work: (1) either the beast human and true human species were formerly even more different from each other than they are now and are in the eons-long process of becoming one species; or (2) the two species started out as one and are in the process of diverging. The first view is called the "Shoemaker Theory," after its primary proponent, Priscilla Shoemaker.* The second viewpoint originated with Ruth Hohrlich, and is called the "Hohrlich Hypothesis."**

Some persons from the scientific sector have offered specious objections to both the Hohrlich and the Shoemaker theories. These would-be scientists claim that, by the very definition of the word "species," separate species cannot interbreed and produce fertile young. This is actually only the usual circumstance. Besides beast human-true human interbreeding, several species of toads are exceptions to this general rule, as are the Mexican swordtail fish and platyfish, who intermate and produce fertile young if members of the opposite sex of their own species are unavailable. In addition, the not infrequent wolf-dog hybrid is fertile. (Figure 6.2)

---

* *See sources listed below.*
1. Shoemaker, Priscilla, "Ancient Sacrificial Rites of *Homo Bestias* as a Probable Contributor to the Merging of Human Types," *Evolution Quarterly,* April-June, 1973.
2. Shoemaker, Priscilla, *The Great Merger: Speculations on the Speciation of Human Types.* (Hilo: Day Press, 1972).
3. Shoemaker, Priscilla, "The Mysterious Disappearance of Atlantis and Its Possible Relation to the Allopatric Speciation of the Genus *Homo,*" *Species,* vol. 31, no. 6, 1974.

** See sources listed below:
1. Hohrlich, Ruth, "The Evolutionary Clock: A Possible Explanation of the Greater Speed of Development of *Homo veridis* as Compared with *Homo bestias,*" *Evolution Quarterly,* vol. 12, no. 2, 1974.
3. Hohrlich, Ruth, "*Homo veridis* or *Homo bestias*: Which Is the Mutant?" *Historical Genetics,* vol. 3, no. 4, 1975.
3. Hohrlich, Ruth, *The Mutation Theory of Human Speciation,* (Seattle, WA: Barry Press, 1972).

Figure 6.2   Although most animals mate only with other members of their own species, exceptions are not unheard of.

The Shoemaker Theory

Shoemaker makes good evolutionary sense by giving the force factor (F.F.) in beast humans primary responsibility for the interspecific disparity in human beings. The beast human's innate preference for using brute force, combined with the degradation compulsion (D.C.), is thought to have impelled him to prefer the more highly evolved females of the true human species to the more beastly females of his own species. Such cross-specific longings are far from uncommon in our own epoch; numbers of rural men have traditionally chosen sheep for sexual companions, and Catherine the Great's lust for horses is said to have led to her untimely death.

Brute force would have enabled the beast human to prevail easily over the true human in competition for the desired females. In this manner, beast human females became less and less frequently mated, as did true human males, who are now on the brink of extinction. The true human female and the beast human male were naturally selected to survive, leaving us in our present quandary.

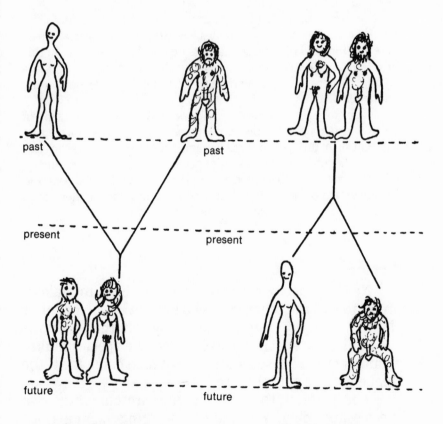

after Shoemaker   after Hohrlich

Figure 6.3

The Hohrlich Hypothesis

Hohrlich's argument is equally compelling. Hohrlicians contend that the force factor (F.F.) in beast humans might well have led the males to select the more refined females within their own species as mates rather than their more bestial sisters. The finer the female, the more likely was she to resist certain advances, thus requiring more force; and the more refined she was, the greater the potential for defilement. The result was that the more highly evolved females within the species were sexually selected over the eons and the more bestial females were deselected.

Similarly, the more bestial males tended to mate more frequently than the less bestial males, because the less bestial males were less inclined to force sexual acts on and defile females. In this way, the more bestial males were naturally selected over their less bestial brothers at the same time that the opposite was happening among females.

Over the ages, the small changes which became evident in males and females as a result of the selection process formed an aggregation of difference of such magnitude that the two sexes can no longer be considered as a single species. This is pure Darwinism, and is the commonly accepted explanation of how the wild boar and the domestic pig, or the wood rat and the house mouse, developed into separate species from a common ancestry.

Summary

Neither theory has a shred of evidence to make it preferable to the other. So, who is right? Shoemaker or Hohrlich? In my opinion, debating whether humans used to be one species or used to be two species makes about as much sense as debating which came first: the chicken or the egg? (Figure 6.4)

The point is that we humans are currently two species, and scientists should be devoting their energies to remedying the situation, not arguing about how it came about.

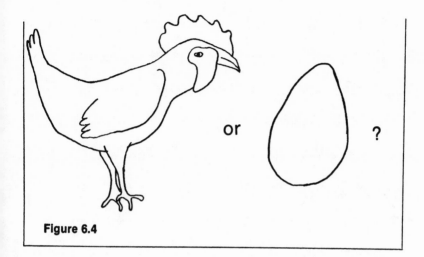

or   ?

Figure 6.4

chapter 7

Philosophers Ponder

No field of study is safe from philosophers. On any college campus you will find them, like poor relations, adopted by each of the various departments: one in education, one in political science, one in linguistics...and on and on. A few of them have come knocking on our door at the Center for the Study of Human Types, and we have done our fair share for this harmless minority group by giving them room and board and pen and paper in exchange for their always voluminous thoughts.

The first thousand pages a philosopher writes are always unclear, incoherent, and completely devoid of value. Occasional interesting thoughts begin to appear in the second and third thousand pages, and—rarely—a practical, empirical idea will emerge somewhere around page 4000. Loretta Monroe's work followed this pattern. She developed an interesting idea which she called "The Propitious-Obligatory Linguistic Dichotomy," renamed "The Get/Have Distinction" by the non-philosophers at the Center.

The Get/Have Distinction

To describe this elegant theory, let me detail a study Monroe conducted at the Center to test it.

Three thousand (3000) males and three thousand (3000) females were selected to answer a confidential questionnaire. Anonymity was assured by having each person detach the required personal data section of the questionnaire and turn it in separately from the questionnaire itself, which was sealed in a blank green envelope for males, orange for females. Confidentiality was thus protected, and all the respondents were able to complete the four items honestly. Here are the test and the results.

The Monroe Test

This test consists of four items. There are two underlined words in the sentence below each test item. Circle the one which more accurately completes the sentence for you.

Item #1. You are employed as an aide by the CIA. Your duties include "romancing" attractive young members of the opposite sex who are suspected of espionage. You must occasionally conduct searches of your lovers' quarters and persons for valuable secrets or goods believed to be in their possession. You are a devoted employee and a loyal citizen.

I get/have to probe for secret documents in the body orifices of suspected spies of the opposite sex.

Results:
females: 2% get to probe; 98% have to probe
males: 97% get to probe; 3% have to probe

Item #2. You are a student in veterinary school. For part of your clinical practice, you must work twenty hours in a large rural veterinary clinic and complete whatever duties the veterinarian in charge assigns to you. A beautiful young race horse is brought in with constipation, and the doctor prescribes an anal purgative.

I get/have to give an enema to a horse.

Results:
females: 8% get to give; 92% have to give
males: 81% get to give; 19% have to give

Item #3. You are a guard in a large penitentiary. The warden does not want a riot in his prison, and believes the best way to prevent such an occurrence is to beat the inmates regularly. You are responsible for administering this preventive measure in your cell block.

I get/have to suppress potential prison rioters with a club.

Results:
females: 0.5% get to suppress; 99.5% have to suppress
males: 89% get to suppress; 11% have to suppress

Item #4. You are working in the testing division of a company that is marketing a new deodorant for athletes. The product is reputed to keep the groin area free of offensive odor even after a three-mile run, and the honesty-in-advertising law requires that the claim be proved. The ten persons completing the run are very attractive members of the opposite sex.

I get/have to sniff underpants worn by members of the opposite sex.

> **Results:**
> females: 4% get to sniff; 96% have to sniff
> males: 91% get to sniff; 9% have to sniff

Clearly, there is a difference between *getting* to do something and *having* to do something. One *gets* to do what is pleasurable; one *has* to do what is unpleasant. Monroe's remarkable study has proved that there is a fundamental difference between what most men (beast humans) find pleasurable and what most women (true humans) find pleasurable. Hence, valuable new evidence for our duo-species theory.

The only person who was not impressed by the outcome of the study was Loretta Monroe, who insisted that if 96% of males are beast humans and 4% are true humans, then 96% of the males in the study should have chosen *get* in all four items, and 4% should have chosen *have* in all four items. Being a philosopher, she believed in the absolute validity of her test and determined to find out why the results did not come out precisely as she had expected.

Monroe took the original personal data sheets which had been detached from the questionnaire and brushed the upper corner of each with a special fluid to reveal a theretofore hidden code number which she matched with the code number of the questionnaire from which it had been detached. Monroe was thus able to quiz every respondent who had given inconsistent answers on the test.

For instance, one man, who had answered "get" on all items except #3, turned out to be a prison guard in real life. He told Monroe that he had enjoyed clubbing prisoners for about twenty years, but had finally grown tired of it. To him, clubbing had become a chore.

Incredibly, *in every case,* Loretta Monroe found that there was some such special circumstance which explained why the respondent had answered differently from what she would have expected. The final figures showed males 96% get, 4% have on all four items.

Finally satisfied with the empirical results, Monroe wrote her theory, which I have tried to faithfully capsulize below.

The Theory

All human behavior can be divided into two categories: (1) that which society approves deriving pleasure from, and (2) that which society disapproves deriving pleasure from. The former, Monroe calls "Class A" behaviors or "Get" behaviors. The latter, she calls "Class B" behaviors or "Have" behaviors. According to Monroe, **the range of "Get" behaviors is much greater for men (beast humans) than it is for women (true humans).** (Figure 7.1)

the set of all human behaviors

$\left(\smile \right)$ = class A

$\left(\frown \right)$ = class B

Figure 7.1   Monroe's Behavior Classification Circle

We "get" to do things that give us pleasure, and we "have" to do things that cause us pain. By the simple substitution of "get" for "have," we form a completely different opinion of the person who utters, "I have to go shoot the crippled horse now." Of course, society somewhat inhibits the free use of these loaded words. For instance, it is generally unacceptable for a person to admit that he likes killing horses, so in our example, he is likely to use "have" even if he has been eagerly looking forward to the opportunity all week. Nonetheless, the usage does reveal what persons are societally permitted to enjoy doing, and there seem to be many more things which men are permitted to enjoy doing than there are things which women are permitted to enjoy doing. A few more get/have examples will clarify this fact.

Example #1. Monica G. has decided that she wishes to have sex with twenty-one males in one night. She also enjoys sex with new men just about every week, generally "picking up" potential partners from the street for this purpose. Such behavior and desire earn Monica the label of "slut" from old-fashioned persons and "sick" from modern, enlightened persons. She earns a number of other labels from old-fashioneds and moderns alike, some of the more printable of which are "unnatural," "unhealthy," and "immoral." *Clearly, Monica is committing Class B behavior.*

Example #2. Peter T., Ron P., Fred L., Bob H., *et al., ad infinitum,* not only serve Monica G., but also try to compete with her record. They usually are not in the same ballpark for number of encounters, but it is not for lack of trying. They too "pick up" total strangers as frequently as possible and engage in a myriad of sexuo-reproductive acts with as many as possible. *This kind of behavior is considered "natural"—definitely Class A.*

Example #3. Veronica G. (Monica's twin sister), is sometimes seized by and succumbs to a desire to insert items such as small gold perfume vials or slender lipstick cases into the rectums of her dates. Veronica has been ostracized by everyone who has learned of this habit. *The behavior is considered very seriously disturbed and extremely Class B.*

Example #4. Monica and Veronica's older brother, Vernon G., on the other hand, enjoys putting everything from M&M's to roll-on deodorant sticks into his dates' body orifices, and all of his friends find his behavior very amusing and perfectly acceptable. *He is committing Class A behavior.*

Example #5. In Gallo, Montana, a seventeen year old cheerleader became overwhelmed with desire in a deserted school hallway when an obviously well-hung sixteen-year-old male athlete entered the hallway on his way to the shower, wearing only his jock strap and gym shorts. The girl grabbed the boy (who was extremely weak after a very arduous basketball practice) and forced him to the floor where she sucked on his penis and subsequently had coitus with him. The girl was not only stripped of her cheerleader status, but was convicted of rape and assault. Her family disowned her, her friends rejected her, and men regarded her as untouchable. What the cheerleader had done, according to the court record was "unnatural, unacceptable, and immoral." *In short, it was Class B.*

Example #6. In a deserted hallway in Minneapolis, a sixteen-year-old boy raped a fifteen-year-old girl who was provocatively dressed, and the judge acquitted the youth of all responsibility on the grounds that he was behaving in a "normal, healthy" manner. *The young man's behavior was Class A.*

Throughout history, men have derived pleasure from performing acts which repulse women. This broader range of acceptable pleasure-producing behavior for male beast humans suggests an innate constitutional weakness, and society holds him no more responsible for this deficiency, or difference, than it holds a person responsible for having epilepsy or a club foot. It would be unkind and unreasonable to do so.

Societal allowances for this difference have become so thoroughly entrenched over the ages that few people are even aware that allowances are being made. If such allowances are pointed out to a woman, she is likely to shrug and say, "Boys will be boys." She couldn't be more right about that fact or more accurate in her description without becoming highly technical.

The Tragic Flaw of the True Human

Mildred Meany was another occupant of the large broom closet that we reserve for philosophers-in-residence at the Center. A part of Meany's work consisted of listening to and reading the records of over 300 miserable true human beings in our Support Center for Intersexually Distressed Women. According to Meany, 89% of the counseling cases fell into one of three basic types, which are illustrated by the following representative case histories.

■ *Type 1*

Florinda L. Florinda's husband (K.) beats her quite frequently. Following each incident, she searches her soul to find the fault or infraction which prompted the beating. Being a true human, she finds a problem and begins working hard to correct it. Although she would prefer that her husband criticize her verbally rather than physically, she considers the stresses and pressures K. works under and the influences and injustices to which he was subjected in his childhood, and she understands and forgives his behavior. Florinda also considers other aspects of K.'s character and concludes that the beatings are delivered by a basically decent man.* She normally concludes her post-beating reverie by comparing K.'s violent expression of displeasure with her own outbursts of temper—such as throwing a damp dishcloth into the sink when she hears the newspaper boy break the front window for the third time in three months. She comes to understand that she and K. simply have different ways of expressing their dissatisfactions and frustrations.

Florinda was given intense psychotherapy in which she was told that: (1) K.'s beatings are in no way related to the imperfections she believes prompts them; (2) K. enjoys beating people and seeing

---

* A slight digression on the topic of this "basic decency" of the beast human is called for. Interviews with past grade school teachers, ministers, and neighbors of rapists and mass murderers almost invariably produce statements that the assailant is a "basically decent" or "deep-down good" person. Perhaps it is time that true humans and beast humans alike began attaching less significance to these basic qualities (assuming there is any reason to believe they exist anyway) and began concentrating on some of the superficial qualities, since it is the superficial ones that seem to govern their behavior.

them cower before him; and (3) K.'s inner governing mechanisms are not like hers, so she must search somewhere other than in her own mind and her own life for explanations of his behavior.

Florinda has been unable to accept these ideas. She is continuing her efforts at self-improvement with admirable diligence. She is anxious and concerned because she cannot seem to make the necessary progress, as evidenced by the frequency of the beatings, which have not diminished. She despairs over her hopeless inadequacy. She wants the marriage to work out. Prognosis: Poor.

■ *Type 2*

Marcella O. Marcella often feels that she's losing her mind. Also, she has pronounced feelings of worthlessness. Marcella lives with her husband A. and her father H. The three of them have discussions almost every night after dinner. Marcella enjoys participating in these discussions and, much to her pleasure, is often allowed to. Usually, her contributions are ignored, but sometimes they are only quickly dismissed. Marcella knows A. and H. would not ignore or dismiss good ideas, so she realizes that all her ideas are bad. The fact that she often feels their contributions are not very good only further attests to the inferiority of her own, because A. and H. rarely dismiss each other's ideas, not even those she finds wholly wrong, and she is certain that if the ideas weren't good ones, they would be dismissed.

All this proves that she doesn't understand what's going on, or A. and H. are far beyond her, so she retires from the discussion so as not to impede its progress. Very often, while she is washing the dishes, the discussion will end with either A. or H. expressing what sounds to Marcella like an idea she contributed earlier (which was dismissed), and the idea is lauded as the "answer" to whatever question was being discussed. It is for this reason that Marcella believes that she is losing her mind.

After careful analysis and extensive therapy which emphasized that some persons cannot tolerate ideas from those they consider inferior or by whom they feel threatened, and that loud voices generally receive more credit than soft ones, Marcella smilingly (she had laughed frequently during therapy sessions; the therapist feels that Marcella may, after all, be losing her mind) thanked the psychiatric team and announced that their ideas didn't make sense to her either. She said that she certainly never would allow a serious discussion to suffer by disregarding any valuable contributions to it and that she knew her husband and father wouldn't either; that since she had evidently given the therapist the mistaken impression that they would, now she realized that she also had a problem in making herself understood in conversation, which compounded her original problem. Marcella has since taken up philosophy in hopes of exercising and toning her mind. Prognosis: Guarded.

■ *Type 3*

Josephine C. Josephine states she was, and still is, deeply in love with S. She describes their eight month relationship as intimate and rewarding, but S. has now left her for another woman, who, he says, is better looking. Josephine is suffering great pain and has many regrets. She knows that S. would not have left her if she had been worthy as a lover; she also knows S. was very worthy as a lover or she would not be so sorry he left. When asked about how S. feels about the situation, Josephine reports that he has told her that he is very fond of her, and that he is very confused about why she seems to be suffering so much, although he has to admit that he is one hell of a guy. Both S. and Josephine are confused: she wonders how the love she knows S. felt for her disappeared so easily; he doesn't know why she's so upset.

Therapy for Josephine consisted primarily of assuring her that there was nothing wrong with her, that she must simply realize that men have very limited emotional capabilities and not blame herself for that fact. Josephine and S. will repeat this scenario several times, with different partners, and will most likely be as bewildered the last time it is played out as they were the first time. Prognosis: Hopeless.

Largely from these records, Mildred Meany formulated her theory of the *Tragic Flaw of the True Human*. According to her, the true human is preordained to a life of misery, weakness, submission, and abuse because of the tragic flaw in her character: her humility.

The tragedy begins in woman's infancy. Mildred posits that infants of all species take for granted that they are of the same species as their other family members and acquaintances. This seems to be true even in those exceptional cases in which the youngster is in fact adopted by a different species—a cat among a litter of dogs, for example.

There are recorded cases of abandoned human babies being found and reared by wolves. These children do not question their identities as wolves; they quite naturally assume they are of the same species as their fellows. (Figure 7.2)

Figure 7.2   A cat reared in a monkey family would quite naturally assume it was a monkey.

Similarly, a female true human instinctively assumes she is of the same species as those who rear her and control her destiny in the world. Her experiences, particularly her education, reinforce this instinctive belief.

With such an assumption, it is easy to see how—through her humility—the true human begins to perceive the beast humans as superior to the true humans. She humbly perceives the complexities of the world and despairs of ever achieving a complete understanding of them. She also notices that beast humans suffer no such self-doubts. She does not realize that beast humans lack all humility and instead are naturally predisposed to have exalted opinions of themselves. Assuming that they are basically like her, she can find no other explanation for their higher self-esteem but that they must really be superior to her. Thus, those who are actually a separate, *higher* species, come to believe, through the flaw of humility, that they are inferior members of the *same* species.

Of course, whether a quality is a flaw or a virtue depends on the surrounding culture. Humility is a flaw only in societies in which the true human co-exists (and co-habits) with creatures who are without humility. Unfortunately, this includes all civilizations in which she has ever existed. Thus, the potential virtue is not only a flaw, but a curse. In a beastly culture, the quality can only work to the great disadvantage, debasement, and abuse of the true humans.

Meany imagines (and it takes a sizeable imagination) a predominantly true human society to see how the quality of humility would fare. Ego, power, and ambition would not determine who governed or who attained influential positions in the professions and trades. Rather, each aspirant (though "aspirant" would not be an accurate term in a true human society; our language is limited by the beastly societies it was developed to describe) would recognize her own limitations and her own strengths and would step aside unhesitatingly to allow for the progress of one more qualified than she for the task at hand.

Unfortunately, since they tragically and wrongfully assume that men are like themselves, many women believe this highly civilized method of selection of exceptional human beings *is* *presently at work* in society. A woman is quick to admit that her boss is in his position because he is simply better at the work than anyone else available; that the president of her children's university is so because he was the best candidate.

In contrast, a beast human will not relinquish a piece of power even if he realizes someone else would be better than he at exercising it. (Of course, it is usually impossible for him even to imagine that anyone else could be better at it.) He lacks the enlightening quality of humility, and this lack works to his very great material and social advantage.

Should all the other characteristics of true humanness be absent, the presence of humility alone would distinguish her from all other species. It is indeed an unfortunate irony of heroic proportion that the most transcendent of all the refined characteristics of true humanness is also the one most responsible for the female's degradation and unhappiness.

When a true human humbly submits to a beast human, the beast human does not see an admirable ceding of power to a believed-to-be superior in her behavior; rather, he perceives that women will put up with almost anything, will accept—and practically encourage—abuse. Regardless of the advantages it could have provided in a true human culture, it is far better to rid women of their humility than to condemn them to continue to suffer its mindless, bestial trampling.

How Can They Be So Blind?

It is understandable that the true human's humble deference to beast humans results from her belief that she and they are members of the same species. But why does she persist in this conviction despite all the evidence to the contrary?

Hybrid Quality. For one thing, the physical indistinguishability of true humans from beast humans is misleading to the true human, making it impossible to identify the other species at the outset of an acquaintanceship. This is one of the primary reasons she remains convinced that men are of the same species as herself. Let's consider an illustration. Have you ever picked up a coconut in the grocery store and been struck by the humanish face it displays? Well if, because of this seeming humanness, you have ever recoiled at the thought of beating a coconut open with a hammer or drilling a hole in it or tossing it down the basement stairs, you can appreciate the feelings of true humans dealing with beast humans, who look even more appealingly human than coconuts. (Figure 7.3)

Figure 7.3   Coconuts present a moral dilemma similar to that presented by beast humans. (Oliver, Lucee, "The Treatment of Coconuts in Three Primitive Societies," *Journal of Morality and Ethics*, March 1980.)

This external appearance, which suggests that true human emotions and sensitivities are right beneath the surface, is unfortunate indeed. After all, one could have few illusions about what to expect from a mate who had a rumpled fleece, long yellow teeth, and a low, menacing growl. This hybrid quality of the beast human is probably second only to the tragic flaw itself as an obstacle to true human enlightenment.

Pack Phenomenon. To complicate matters even more, a woman who is habitually alone with her man is lulled into believing that his character and beliefs are more truly human than she might otherwise think, because beast humans tend to imitate the behavior of those they are around, much as monkeys do. The first time a woman sees her man in the company of other beast humans, she is likely to be greatly shocked.

What is it that shocks her? Like other predatory species, the beast human has a pack identity which is very different from his individual identity. Once in his pack, the animal's voice becomes raspier, and he speaks more frequently on crass subjects; a mildly crazed look enters his eye, and the eye often reddens a bit; all of his manners and words become tainted with lasciviousness (even such neutral sentences as, "Please pass the butter" can make a true human blush with shame); the lips become moister, and bits of drool may escape at the corners; he emits an almost imperceptible odor, which makes a non-pack member uneasy. The symptoms are often so mild that only a trained observer can spot them; the untrained observer senses the totality of the change, but cannot usually isolate its individual components.

The female true human is ordinarily ignorant of the pack identity, and its discovery is a very painful and traumatic experience. She excuses and explains the newly discovered behavior in a number of true human ways. She convinces herself that her beloved behaves this way because he has to be accepted by his peers, and they are less refined than he; that these qualities really are not in conflict with the others she believed he had, but are simply his "manliness" coming through; that the humidifier is turned too high, and the bathroom needs cleaning.

Because of their blindness, true humans continue to attach themselves to beast humans, and continue to submit to and pay homage to them. The commonly heard query, "What does she see in *him?"* can usually be answered in a word: "Nothing!" but "What is she hoping to find in him?" would deserve a pathetically long answer, including many of the human qualities she assumes he must have, because he is, she naively assumes, a true human, like herself.

Is There Any Hope?

Mildred Meany's philosophical analysis of women's lives accurately described the causes of their misery, but gave no hint of a remedy. And, in fact, we had already tried every conventional therapy technique to help these very unhappy women, to no avail. Still, we did not want to give up.

We decided to run a large advertisement in the most widely circulated newspapers and magazines in Nebraska, requesting women who were leading happy personal lives to get in touch with us. Six hundred and twelve (612) women responded to the advertisement, ninety-three (93) of whom were beast humans. What was the secret of the other 519? Could we discover it, and from it develop a radical new therapy which might work in cases where all other techniques had failed?

The secret was easy to discover. All 519 of the women were lesbians. Our course was clear: we needed to lesbianize our clients.

I flew to Atlanta to visit the highly successful Lesbian Preschool Project, a radical nursery school for two to four-year-old girls. The curriculum is designed to prevent heterosexuality, nip it in the bud before it can blossom. Marianne Silversmith and Belynda Jung, Co-Directors of the school, introduced me to some of the techniques they employed with pre-lesbian preschoolers.

For example, I saw the beautiful, plush "woman" doll named "Yummy" made of velvet and satin which the girls got to handle and take naps with when they behaved appropriately. And I saw the ugly "man" doll named "Yucky" made of burlap and steel wool which the girls had to play with when they did not perform satisfactorily. (Figure 7.4)

Sometimes the teachers put little pools of egg whites into the

Figure 7.4   "Yummy" and "Yucky"

girls' beds at nap time. When the children rolled over into the mess and complained, a teacher would say, "Oh, *icky!* A *man* must have been in that bed. Oh, *ugh, nasty, ick!* That only happens when a *man* gets into your bed."

I saw enough to convince me that the creative women who developed this program were exactly the people I needed to design my lesbianization program in Bleeding Heart, so I made Marianne and Belynda an offer they couldn't refuse, and we all flew back to Nebraska together.

Wasting no time, Marianne Silversmith and Belynda Jung sent out their first wave of information packets to our therapy clients only a week after their arrival at the Center. The packets contained the following form letter.

SAVE THE WOMEN!

Dear Woman:

We are distressed to note from the information contained in your personal file at the Center for the Study of Human Types that you suffer from a malady called <u>heterosexuality</u>.

We are conducting a pilot project to develop and implement techniques for bringing relief to the millions of women who suffer from this ailment, and invite you to participate in the project as an experimental subject.

Please read the enclosed fact sheet about the heartache of heterosexuality, and then return the enclosed postpaid card to reserve a place in our therapy program.

Sincerely,

Marianne Silversmith
Marianne Silversmith
Chief Therapist

Belynda Jung

Belynda Jung
Coordinator

The fact sheet mentioned above follows.

Answers to the Six Most Often Asked Questions About Heterosexuality

Q.: **What is heterosexuality?**
A.: Heterosexuality is a disease characterized by the desire for intimate physical connection with a person or persons not of your gender.
Q.: **What causes heterosexuality?**
A.: No one knows exactly what causes heterosexuality. There is reason to believe that there are several different causes. There seems to be a genetic predisposition to heterosexuality in certain families. Environmental factors either cause or contribute to some cases of heterosexuality. There is no evidence that heterosexuality is transmitted via public toilets.
Q.: **Who gets heterosexuality?**
A.: Heterosexuality strikes nine out of ten Americans. About 10% of the population appears to have a natural immunity to the disease. Heterosexuality strikes people of every socio-economic class, race, and religion. Heterosexuality is usually contracted in early childhood, and, if untreated, lasts a lifetime.
Q.: **Is heterosexuality fatal?**
A.: Not usually. The average life expectancy for heterosexuals is about one and one-half years shorter than for homosexuals. Childbirth used to be the most frequent cause of death directly attributable to heterosexuality, but modern obstetric methods have greatly reduced this risk. The biggest killer now is the IUD (intrauterine device), followed closely by The Pill and enraged husbands. Still, chances of survival are excellent.
Q.: **Can heterosexuality be prevented?**
A.: Not yet, but research on a vaccine is promising. It is hoped that an injectible serum, manufactured from the tissues of healthy, i.e. homosexual, donors, will provide lifetime protection from heterosexuality in children under the age of six.
Q.: **Is there a cure for heterosexuality?**
A.: No, heterosexuality cannot usually be cured. But there is a very effective treatment which so completely controls the symptoms of heterosexuality that nearly complete, permanent remission of the disease is possible.

No, There Is No Hope

Two hundred and eighteen (218) women—about 60% of those receiving the packets—participated in the SAVE THE WOMEN experiment. Unfortunately, after scarcely six months, Marianne and Belynda handed me their resignation. It read, in part:

> The heart of our preventive program with preschoolers was aversive stimulation. These unfortunate heterosexual women have already been subjected to and have withstood far more aversive conditions than we would ever dream of simulating in the clinic. Where beatings, rapes, and other inhuman abuse have failed to deter these women from consorting with men, what chance of success have we with our egg whites, sandpaper dummies, and short-circuited vibrators?...this job is much more difficult than we had envisioned...wish you the very best at developing an effective program under new directors...firm, personal belief that these women are hopelessly heterosexual and beyond help.

We have discontinued the program.

chapter 8

Bringing Out the Beast

We have seen that (1) there are two human species and that (2) the dual species existence is intolerable. Now we come to the question of how to resolve the situation. In theory, there are three alternatives: (1) segregation; (2) humanization; (3) bestialization.

Segregation

Some persons have suggested that segregation of the two sexes/species would be the most humane, practical, and in all ways preferable solution to our problem. Admittedly, the mechanics of segregation are immensely simpler than the mechanics of the other two alternatives. This solution is, however, a much more difficult one overall because the resistance to it by all concerned—male and female, beast human and true human—is so very powerful.

For instance, read the files of the Dean of Students of any all-men's or all-women's college in the country. You will find dozens of examples of seemingly intelligent young people jeopardizing their personal reputations, their opportunities for various honors and scholarships, their very college careers to mingle with the opposite sex. With admirable resourcefulness, these young people have been known to smuggle themselves in and out of each other's dormitories in laundry carts, scale hundred-foot walls on ropes made of neckties, hide for hours at a time all folded up in closets while suspicious proctors make room searches. No matter how stringent the rules, no matter how powerful the authorities, no matter how dire the penalties, these students find ways of accomplishing forbidden intersexual meetings.

In fact, the greater the risks and obstacles to their meeting, the more ardent human animals become, both beast and true. Pyramus and Thisbe, Romeo and Juliet...How many famous lovers would never have loved had they not been forbidden to do so? Until a cure for heterosexuality is found, the prospects for voluntary segregation of the species are dim, at best.

Prisons provide the only really successful example of the sexes in segregation. One of my colleagues, Paulina Zitherspoon, is so impressed with prison life that she has written a very original tract calling for imprisonment of the entire human population. (Paulina spent fourteen years in various prisons for some problems she had writing checks and using cars that didn't belong to her.) As she points out, both men and women adjust readily to prison life. Women, she claims, talk, read, and do needlework. Men, when they realize there won't be any women around, rape, beat, and kill one another instead.

Although there is much to be said in favor of Zitherspoon's plan, I'm afraid it is not politically feasible. There is little chance that a majority of the population would vote to put themselves in prison.

Given the insurmountable problems with implementing a separatist plan, we are forced to abandon the theoretically attractive alternative of segregation.

Humanization

Humanization was tried once before and met with a degree of failure unprecedented in the history of science. The Great Victorian Experiment, as scholars refer to the second half of the 19th century in England, was a grand effort to fully humanize the male population.

Superficially (note the frequent recurrence of this word), men did appear to make great strides toward true humanization. They initiated courtships in a respectful and thoughtful manner; they acknowledged that a single, monogamous love relationship was inherently superior to a string of promiscuous liaisons; they accepted the virtue of sexual purity to be desirable for both sexes. In short, they made a valiant effort to repress their bestiality and to develop their true humanity.

But it did not work. Behind the scenes and after the polite encounters, they consumed pornography and visited brothels more frequently and earnestly than ever before or since. It seems that there is a predetermined amount of bestiality which the beast human must express, and if it is denied expression in one area of his life, it will erupt somewhere else. Bestiality in the beast human is like a dollar bill in the pocket of a gambler; it must be spent.

It is no accident that so many of the romantic novels of today which incorporate the fantasy of the evolved male are set in Victorian times; never before or since has the fantasy been taken so seriously; never before or since has there been such a seeming abundance of evolved males in existence. But it was all a sham, just as today's soap operas, magazines, and movies are shams. Try as they or we will to prove otherwise, the male beast human is beastly, and constitutionally incapable of true humanness.

If a rapprochement between the species is to be effected, it will have to come from the other direction. That is the last alternative.

Figure 8.1   Bestialization

Bestialization

The only tenable approach is the undevelopment, or bestialization, of the true human female. Of course, thousands will clamor that this solution should not under any circumstances be undertaken. There are always those who prefer the status quo, no matter how dire, to change. They will view the true human species as a noble monument to the potential of the evolutionary process, and would have the species continue to suffer the outrages perpetrated by a beastly culture rather than have it altered or tampered with in any way, even for its own benefit.

This view is at once sentimental and callous. I have no objection whatsoever to the construction of a *real* monument, a grand memorial complete with the Grave of the Unknown True Human, as a tribute to the existence of the true human species. But I could never ask unhappy living creatures to sacrifice their own chances for happiness in order that the world could have them as a monument, when the very instrument for their deliverance is within our grasp.

Make no mistake. I too regret the passing of this ill-timed glory of evolution, but my concern for human happiness overwhelms my selfish impulse toward preservation. I, for one, will sleep more easily without the suffering of these millions on my conscience. Naturally, a few should be left in their natural state as specimens for the zoological gardens of the world.

Bestialization Is Egalitarian

Some women will be inclined to hold fast to their true humanness, no matter how much anguish and disharmony it brings to their own lives and the world. Such evolutionary snobbery is regrettable.

Personally, I am attracted to all species without   ception with an absolute fairness and sense of equality. Some of my favorite individuals are not even vertebrates. And if the love of my life were a snail, I would cheerfully relinquish not only my true humanness, with all its regal trappings, but my primateness, vertebrateness, and all the rest, if it were in my power, to balance our abilities and equalize our feelings. So long as I stubbornly refused to step down from my evolutionary pedestal, could the snail and I expect anything but pain, frustration, and confusion in our relationship?

Most of us are fortunate (though it is not a matter of pure chance, as is probably clear by now) in that our loves are among the beast humans, so our metamorphosis need not be quite so drastic. Assuming the correctness of the Hohrlich Hypothesis, bestialization is, after all, merely a regaining of our natural heritage; the bestiality is in us—it only wants awakening. And if the Shoemaker Theory is correct, bestialization is our natural destiny; the true human species is being naturally deselected, so we would only be assisting nature.

Bestialization Is Natural

We have not talked much about natural selection and deselection, but a few thoughts on the topic are appropriate here. For a detailed account of what is meant by "natural selection," I refer my readers to Mr. Charles Darwin's works on the subject. For an understanding of "natural deselection," I again refer my readers to Mr. Darwin, but this time to the man rather than to his works.

Mr. Darwin was a very sickly man, and had it not been for the devoted solicitude of his loving wife, he might well not have made it to old age. I have nothing but praise for Mrs. Darwin for taking such good care of the treasure that was hers (for so she seems to have regarded him), as the world might not otherwise have benefited from the work of this pioneer.

However, I could wish that Mrs. Darwin had exercised a bit more self-control in the love she felt for her husband. It was obvious from his chronic ill health that Mr. Darwin was being naturally deselected; he was not fit to survive. I do not mean, of course, that his end should have been hastened or even that artificial obstacles to his timely passing, such as a doting wife, should not have been employed. I mean merely that once the handwriting is on the wall—once it becomes obvious that one is being deselected—one has an obligation to assist nature by not perpetuating one's ill-fit self in offspring.

An occasional slip-up is understandable, but Mr. and Mrs. Darwin produced seven children. If they had taken some precautions, instead of resisting nature, nature would have needed fewer generations to finish deselecting the Darwins.

Perhaps it is unfair to expect more of Mr. and Mrs. Darwin than we do of others in this regard, but they could have provided a praiseworthy example for others. Instead, they chose to set an absolutely disgraceful precedent for later generations.

Now we are faced with genetic engineers who threaten to decide for us who should be deselected and who should not. If we put the problem into the hands of these specialists, we risk all sorts of mistakes and arbitrariness. But if instead we can convince the world population of the reasonableness of Voluntary Deselection Assistance (VDA; not associated in any way with Venereal Disease Anonymous), there will be no need for the genetic engineers to begin tampering with things.

Be honest with yourself. If you suspect you are in the process of being deselected (e.g. if you are sickly, always with something new; if you are small for your age...), talk it over with a friend, if you have one, or with your pastor or psychiatrist. Don't pretend you don't see the signs. Being deselected is nothing to be ashamed of. It has happened in the best of families and species. It happens to us all in some generation or other.

Bestialization Is Easy

The most glaringly superior, or the most highly evolved, aspect of the female true human is her emotional capacity. If this capacity could be destroyed or removed, most of the other differences between males and females would be negligible. The problem, of course, lies in determining exactly where in the female anatomy the emotional nugget is located so surgeons can pluck it out.

I predict that someday bestialization of newborn girls will be as routine as circumcision of newborn boys is today. But until science has answered the questions: "Where is the higher nature of the true human housed?" and "How can it be excised?" women must, instead, drop themselves into proverbial Skinner boxes until all their higher behaviors have been extinguished and replaced with lower, manlier substitutes.

The transformation should be gradual, like dieting. The way to take off forty pounds is not to cut off your legs, or even to give up eating, but to follow a slow, sensible, medically-approved regimen. Likewise, in removing forty spiritual and emotional pounds, a too vigorous beginning can be discouraging—and sometimes even disastrous—in its results. Tenacity and patience, rather than eagerness and energy, are the keys to success.

Your first step is to determine that you are, positively, a true human, and therefore a candidate for bestialization. If you have any doubt about what species you belong to, take a minute to answer the questions in the following quiz.

Assessing Your Evolutionary Status

1. To which of the following activities would you look forward with the sweetest anticipation?
   (a) having a bowel movement
   (b) a weekend with a sleek, well-muscled wolfhound
   (c) killing deer
   (d) attending a concert
2. If left unexpectedly alone in a snowbound cabin with only books for diversion, which of these titles would you pick up first?
   (1) *Master Without Pity*
   (2) *Hungry Cunts on the Prowl*
   (3) whichever had the best pictures
   (4) *Favorite Love Ballads*
3. You are offered a large, greasy roast pig for dinner. What would you most like to do with it?

    (a) nibble on the well-crisped ears, snout, and tail
    (b) sink your teeth into the nice, meaty rump
    (c) let it cool off enough to fuck it before carving it
    (d) eat the apple from the mouth
4. In a hotel room in a strange city, which movie would you choose to see?
    (a) "Tight Sphincter"
    (b) "Lunatic With a Cleaver"
    (c) "The Swedish Maid and the Magnificent Stallion"
    (d) "Eroticism in Medieval Art"
5. Which would you most like to watch?
    (a) two people copulating
    (b) a woman sucking on a tall, hairy man's penis
    (c) a man cornholing a German shepherd which is mauling a woman in chains
    (d) the balcony scene from *Romeo and Juliet*
6. Whose farts do you enjoy smelling?
    (a) only your own
    (b) your own and those of close friends
    (c) I never smelled one I didn't like
    (d) *Enjoy* smelling farts?
7. Your local community center offers adult education courses, and you decide to enroll in one, mostly to make new friends. Which would you choose?
    (a) Making Beer at Home
    (b) How to Worm a Cat
    (c) Hunting Small, Defenseless Animals for Fun and Profit
    (d) Harvesting Wild Mushrooms, Berries, and Herbs
8. Which setting would you prefer for a tryst with your lover?
    (a) a pick-up truck/camper on a deserted country road
    (b) a motel room with X-rated movies
    (c) the beer-drenched floor of your favorite tavern
    (d) a warm meadow overlooking the sea
9. You want to buy an extra special gift for your lover's birthday. Which would you choose?
    (a) a rainbow assortment of tight, skimpy underpants
    (b) a generously padded lace bra or jock strap
    (c) a handsomely gift-boxed set of jeweled sexual aids (vibrator, French tickler, anal beads)
    (d) satin sheets and pillowcases

10. What do you appreciate most about public toilets?
    (a) the graffiti
    (b) the sounds
    (c) the odors
    (d) the convenience

Scoring. Give yourself 20 points for every (c) answer, 10 points for every (b) answer, 5 points for every (a) answer, and no (0) points for every (d) answer. Use the following table to interpret your score.

0	Unquestionably true human. You need help desperately.
5-50	Tendency toward true humanness; should strongly consider bestialization.
55-100	Fairly well-adjusted
105-195	Supremely well-adjusted
200	We can use you as a Bestialization Program Instructor.

Beginning Bestialization

We offer a bestialization program for true humans at the Center for the Study of Human Types. As an Equal Opportunity Agency, we serve persons of all races and religions, as well as all lifestyles and philosophies. We have treated Communists, Libertarians, and Republicans; vegetarians, carnivores, and omnivores; geniuses, morons, and imbeciles; heterosexuals, homosexuals, bisexuals, and omnisexuals; the sane and the lunatic. We serve any true human in need, regardless of ability to pay, and are on the waiting list for United Way funds, and the longer waiting list for HEW matching funds.

All of our clients are, of course, true human, and over 99% of them are heterosexual women. Three heterosexual women, in dire need of feeling like "one of the boys," have received bestialization treatment. One lesbian elected the treatment because she was, much to her own bewilderment, hopelessly in love with a beast human female. One gay man, who had the most profoundly sad countenance I have ever seen, received treatment, and for the first time in his life feels that he *belongs* in some segment of the human population.

I realize that not everyone can make the pilgrimage to Bleeding Heart, and, also, the waiting list for treatment is long. For those who wish to try self-bestialization instead, I offer the following program, a kind of correspondence course. Although written with a heterosexual female in mind, any true human, regardless of gender or sexual orientation, can easily adapt the suggestions to suit his or her own needs.

The Bestialization Program. An understanding of the nature of sexual love is the first prerequisite to the bestializing process. The true human knows, instinctively, that sexual love, like friendship or maternal love, either happens or doesn't happen. It cannot be taught or learned, nor can it occur with very many persons—ideally, no more than one—in a lifetime. It suffers from (that is, becomes progressively more bestial as a result of) too much practice, experimentation, and efforts at improvement.

Chastity is an important prerequisite to the development of true sexual love, as is ignorance. The potential for true sexual love is diminished by each sexual encounter and fantasy that is not loveful. Ergo: The true human who wishes to become bestial should engage in sexual activities with great frequency and with a wide variety of partners, preferably from about the age of twelve.

Sexual technique should be a requirement in the curriculum of all public junior high schools and should include specific instruction in the use of sexual aids. Related topics, such as anatomy, reproduction, contraception, abortion, VD, and sexual first aid should be included, and the now popular "Family Living" courses abolished.

It is a national disgrace that many female high school graduates don't even know how to use a vibrator for orgasmic release. Until such rudimentary skills are a part of every human female's basic repertoire, the cause of pan-bestialization will be greatly handicapped.

Every young woman should keep a diary as a lasting memento of her initiation into full sexual maturity and activity, much as many young true humans now keep dried flowers from the prom, "love" letters and the like. Appropriate entries would include her first experiences with a new coital position, the length of her orgasms, and anecdotes on her first bout with VD.

Inspirational reading should be included in the course work, such as *One Woman Alone,* the biography of the martyred Felicia M. Goodwin, whose allergy to penicillin made her a sexual cripple for life.

After the young teenager has attended and participated in six or seven orgies, experimented with straight and gay sex, and practiced the Kamasutra with a number of different partners, she will begin to develop her own sexual style and also become divested of such true human impediments as modesty, shyness, and romantic illusions. As she gains proficiency, she will learn which acts and positions result in the most intense orgasms, which tend to prolong excitation, and so forth.

By the time she is in her upper teens, a girl will know exactly what is available in terms of penile length, circumference, and hardness, and will be unlikely to let some romantic notion about a particular partner allow her to overlook a deficiency. In short, she will be very much like her male counterpart. She will climax easily; she will desire and enjoy variety, both in sexual activity and partners; she will appreciate stimulating and revealing clothing that emphasizes the roundness of the testicles or the size of the penis or the cleft of the buttocks; she will delight her friends with detailed descriptions of her sexual forays; and she will enjoy the convenience of being able to minister to her sexual needs, whether close to home, away on business, or wherever. She will be capable of the adult, normal, natural, healthy sex life from which beast humans have benefited for so long, and which has heretofore been denied the frustrated, neurotic, emotional female with her myriad romantic hang-ups.

In addition to this basic understanding of the nature of sexual love, and especially for those who are already past the impressionable age at which the tide of true humanness is most readily reversed, the following specific suggestions are offered.

Step 1

1. External and Superficial Items

■ *Sighs.* Replace all sighs with grunts. This is particularly important during lovemaking (called "sexual activity," or more commonly "fucking" after bestialization). Sighs betray the presence of high and complicated emotions. When these emotions are either forced into inexpression or are greatly lowered and simplified in expression, the utterer has made her first assault on the feelings themselves; they are weakened. Gain complete control of sighs before moving on to *Tears*. If sighs are still slipping out occasionally, and concentration alone cannot seem totally to extinguish them, purchase of an electro-shock machine may be worthwhile. Learn to grunt whenever you feel like being expressive of anything not specifically verbal.

■ *Tears*. Tears cannot be tolerated. Although they are not ordinarily so frequent as sighs, they are more difficult to control, and progress will be slow. When the urge to cry begins to take hold, twist your mouth into a sneer and grunt. Here is where your grunting practice will pay off. This technique has a remarkable way of hardening the impulse to cry, and is the first step in transforming it into a sensori-neural callous.

■ *Gentleness*. Gentleness is inappropriate. Again, in love-making (or fucking, depending on your degree of progress), it should be particularly avoided. Grab when you feel like caressing; scratch rather than rub; bite, don't kiss. This may seem quite unnatural and unsavory at first, but it is not nearly so difficult to accomplish as stopping sighs and tears. You will be expressing yourself in a way your mate will understand, and his happy grunts will reassure you in your approach and progress.

■ *Vocabulary*. You must completely rout certain loaded words and phrases from your vocabulary. Do not allow yourself names or labels for your high instincts and impulses. Once a quality no longer has a name, it is difficult, and eventually impossible, even to think about, let alone desire, that quality. We're talking here about words like "love," "devotion," "trust,"...you know the ones. Substitute a hard core of words like "lust," "physically compatible," "sissy,"...again, you know the ones. Some have argued that the beast human gets to use the first type of word, so giving those words up seems like an unnecessary sacrifice for the true human. But one must remember that beast humans are incapable of experiencing the feelings these words describe, so beast human usage of them is a very different matter from true human usage. Loaded words activate the very delicate trigger of the true human emotional network, so the very quality itself is conjured instantly in her active mind upon hearing the vocabulary.

It is sometimes helpful for true humans at this step to remind themselves that this vocabulary is not lost to them forever; its use is only suspended until bestialization is complete, at which time women are free to re-learn the words. It is interesting, however, that a recent survey of graduates from a program similar to this one revealed that not a single bestialized true human chose to recover the lost words. The general feeling was that there are enough synonyms in English without burdening one's mind with more. If you already know "lust," what use have you for "love?"

Step 2

2. Internal Items.

After completion of Step 1, these modifications will not be nearly so difficult to effect as they will seem to a true human on first reading.

■ *Brutalization of Ideas.* When you are feeling "good," do not allow yourself to think or daydream. Keep very busy at a disagreeable task until the mood passes. Then release your mind to do its work. It will, when allowed freedom only at such times, begin to form predictable patterns of producing mean ideas and mechanical thoughts, devoid of the finer varieties of true human feeling. Practice until habitual. Eventually, this type of thought process will fill your mind even when you feel "good." You will be excitingly close to beastliness when this occurs.

■ *Reconstruction of Mental Images.* Become a Martin Luther with your own mind. Sit quietly and mentally picture your ideal images of love and companionship and related states; then, one by one, take mental sledge hammers and shatter your images. Do a thorough job of pulverizing the pieces so that the debris will not be recognizable or reminiscent of any past attachment should you stumble upon any of it in the future. Since it is hard for beast humans and true humans alike to live with no idols at all, we recommend forming a few golden calves after the destruction.

■ *Dream Control.* Ordinarily, dream control is a pretty automatic aftermath of brutalizing ideas and reconstructing mental images. However, no matter how thorough your work, there are usually a few remote strongholds of true humanness in the less accessible dream centers. In time, this true human-tinged dream matter will become harmless; the bestialized human female will no longer be capable of experiencing the true human qualities portrayed. But, in the newly bestialized human, where the memory can still be activated to recall the dream matter in its past context, real distress and harm can result.

To guard against this possibility, it is advisable during the first six months of bestialization to eat bedtime snacks like pizza, pickles, and onions—whatever foods have caused nightmares and fitful sleep for you as a true human. Several metamorphees have reported great success with dog food. A cup and a half or so about thirty minutes before retiring is believed to be not so disturbing to one's rest as spicier foods, but just as destructive to true human-mattered dream content.

Step 3

■ *Choosing a Practice Mate.* Obviously, a female true human can accomplish bestialization only with the aid of a male beast human. There would be no way to practice, nor any way to measure progress, without coupling.

Therapy must proceed with a practice mate whom you dislike in order to prevent the interference of romantic illusions. With no prior attachment or affection, you will not fear experimentation. You will have nothing to lose except, of course, your true human-ness, which is the whole point. There will be no initial pain from relinquishing unrealistic, romantic notions about how it "might have been" between you. There will be no illusions to dispel about there being finer qualities present than there really are. And finally, practicing with a loathsome mate provides a real test of whether the technique is working, because, if it is, you will find yourself becoming attracted to some of the very qualities you formerly thought disgusting.

First Fruits of Bestialization

Many persons are skeptical about the entire idea of female bestialization, and even more so about our techniques for bringing it about. But the program does work. In 1968, under the direction of BST (Beast Seminar Training), an experimental group of 700 women underwent a bestialization course very much like the one presented above. It was no coincidence that the first woman in history was added to the FBI's "Ten Most Wanted Fugitives" list in that same year. Bestialization spread like wildfire. Four women made the coveted FBI list in 1970, and the Uniform Crime Report indicates that female criminality continues to rise at an astonishing rate.

The adherents of Transcendental Meditation believe that only 1% of the population meditating has a beneficial, calming effect on the whole of society, not just on the meditators. I believe the same phenomenon holds true for female bestialization. Even bestializing less than 1% of the true human population has had a debasing, coarsening effect on the whole of society, not just on the new beast humans.

As an example, look at how reading tastes have changed with the advent of artificial bestialization. At one time, *Cosmo* had a corner on the entire beast human female reading audience, but in the last ten years, a number of more graphic competitors have appeared, most notably, *Playgirl*. And when greater numbers of true humans become bestialized, increasingly explicit magazines will undoubtedly spring up to cater to their more bestial tastes.

The magazines are only one example of many. Droves of women are now clamoring for the most bestial jobs: in the military, on police forces and road gangs, as professional athletes, and even— as an indication of the complete deterioration of the true human fiber—as lawyers. A mere 9% of all law students were female in 1972. That figure rose to an astounding 23% in only three years, a clear indication of the deep social inroads bestialization is paving.

Far from unbestializable, the true human female population is on the very brink of the bestial dawn, and the first brave subjects have shown the way to the rest of us.

Conclusion

I find myself in a predicament similar to Dr. B.F. Skinner's: I have the means for producing greater happiness in the world, but people's stubborn refusal to relinquish their mistaken impressions of what is valuable or good presents a serious obstacle. Freedom and dignity, refinement and virtue—all such true human qualities impede our regression into a more harmonious existence. Until people can disabuse themselves of their illusions about the inherent desirability of being true human, Dr. Skinner and I will both face grave difficulties.

Fundamental changes in society are always slow, but when the new dawn breaks on the new world in which we all will have, in a sense, been born again, the wait and the struggle will seem but two flecks of dust in a cloudless, sunny sky.